D0803895

A Healing Walk with St. Ignatius

Discovering God's Presence in Difficult Times

WITHDRAWN
Wilmette Public Library

WILMETTE PUBLIC LIBRARY
1242 WILMETTE AVENUE
WILMETTE, IL 60091
847-256-5025

A HEALING WALK WITH ST. IGNATIUS

Discovering God's Presence in Difficult Times

LYN HOLLEY DOUCET

LOYOLAPRESS.
CHICAGO

WILMETTE PUBLIC LIBRARY

LOYOLAPRESS.

3441 N. ASHLAND AVENUE
CHICAGO, ILLINOIS 60657

© 2002 Lyn Holley Doucet
All rights reserved

Scripture quotations are from the New Jerusalem Bible © 1985 by Darton, Longman & Todd, Ltd., and Doubleday, a division of Bantam Doubleday Dell Publishing Group, Inc. Reprinted by permission.

"Heart of My Own Heart" © 2000, Christopher Walker. Published by OCP Publications, 5536 NE Hassalo, Portland OR 97213. All rights reserved. Used with permission.

"Make Us Holy Make Us Whole" Mark Friedman/Janet Vogt. © 1998 Unity Music Press, a division of The Lorenz Corporation.

Picture credit: © Maria Muller/Graphistock

Interior design by Nick Panos

Library of Congress Cataloging-in-Publication Data

Doucet, Lyn Holley, 1950–
  A healing walk with St. Ignatius : discovering God's presence in difficult times / Lyn Holley Doucet.
      p. cm.
Includes bibliographical references.
  ISBN 0-8294-1988-8
  1. Suffering—Religious aspects—Catholic Church. 2.
Healing—Religious aspects—Catholic Church. 3. Ignatius, of Loyola,
Saint, 1491-1556. 4. Christian life—Catholic authors. I. Title.
  BX2373.S5 D68 2003
  248.8'6—dc21

2002151710

Printed in the United States
02 03 04 05 06 Bang 10 9 8 7 6 5 4 3 2 1

248.86
DO

*For my parents, Minnetta & J. B. Holley
and for Mrs. Elva McCann Humphries,
my eighth-grade teacher, who read
my compositions aloud to the class.*

TABLE OF CONTENTS

They wanted to follow Jesus, but in the footsteps of Iñigo, in the same way one might do when he places his foot in the imprint left on the snow by someone who has gone ahead of him.

JOSÉ IGNACIO TELLECHEA IDÍGORAS,
Ignatius the Pilgrim Saint

INTRODUCTION

The lesson which he gives is interior consolation; this dispels all confusion and draws a person to every kind form of love of the Lord. In this consolation to some persons he gives light, and to others he reveals many secrets, and so forth. . . . This consolation points out and opens for us the path we should follow.
St. Ignatius of Loyola, in a letter to Teresa Rejadell

As I take my morning walk, I ponder this introduction. How can I express the purpose of this book? What does the reader need to know before beginning it?

It is a blue and gold day in south Louisiana, now in the cherished fall season, when the humidity abates and the temperature lowers. I fold my arms to clasp my red sweatshirt closer because the wind is surprisingly sharp. As I walk, I crunch a bumper crop of acorns under my feet. Four boys fly by on bikes and scooters, waving good morning. A large dog looms close by, and I turn quickly and walk away from his steely blue eyes. An old man cordially lifts his hat to me; he is one of a dying breed. Cars turn into the church parking lot, where doors slam as people hurry in. Walks have often seemed to me slices of life that represent the whole of life. They represent especially the spiritual journey, that journey about which I now write.

For some years I have reflected on this question: How does a healing God work in the lives of wounded people? And because we are all wounded in some way, this question becomes: How is

God's grace at work in people's lives? The more I search out answers, of course, the more questions arise. This is as it should be. All efforts to fully understand God's ways must end in enduring mystery. As the great writer Paul Tillich said, "For who can possess God?"

Yet I cannot ignore the patterns and truths I see emerging in the lives of those I interview. Perhaps exploring these patterns— through stories—will help others. First, it seems that God requires the surrender of our will to his will. Only then can God work in the ways he wants. Whether this surrender is easy or hard, it must occur or God's ways are thwarted. Second, God works healing in each life differently. Each person is unique, and each journey to God and healing is different, as illustrated by the stories to follow. Third, God seems to reach out to us in our darkest hour, often when we are in the throes of passionate despair. Yes, he certainly comes quietly to quiet hearts, but often the intensity of our feelings draws his ardent grace directly to us.

Last, and much to the point in this book, the search that others have made for God—and their experiences with God—can benefit us today on our own journeys. For although we are different, we are paradoxically much the same; we are a broken, pilgrim people whose hearts are hungry until they rest in God.

One of the wisest of pilgrims was St. Ignatius of Loyola. Several years ago, with the help of Jesuit friends, I began studying St. Ignatius, a sixteenth-century Basque nobleman who surrendered all to God. It is a blessing that much of his wisdom has survived in written form and has made its way into our modern world.

Ignatius was a man of extremes. In his life, status and wealth contrasted with humiliation and poverty. Power and worldly ambition were replaced by imprisonment and torturous doubt. Royal comfort turned to deprivation and illness. Yet throughout his life, some things did not change. He had a courageous and chivalrous heart. He longed to do great deeds for those whom he followed. He was steadfastly loyal to friends and comrades, even unto death. Strength of purpose and boldness of action were always present in Ignatius of Loyola.

God worked with these very aspects of Ignatius's personality to transform him from haughty knight to humble saint. Along his rocky way, Ignatius developed a deep and shared wisdom. He became a genius of Christian practice, and his words are timeless.

In this book you will find the words and deeds of service of St. Ignatius of Loyola coupled with true, modern stories of brokenness, healing, and endurance—physical, spiritual, and psychological. His words are applied to the issues and principles of each story. I have provided you, as readers, with questions for journaling and reflection so that similar issues in your own lives might take on new clarity. There are also suggestions on page 221 for using this book in a prayer group or similar gathering. Being with a group of like-minded, supportive friends can be a great help along our spiritual journey.

As we walk through this book together, I hope that it may lead to our understanding ourselves better and, in turn, understanding our place in Christ's kingdom of love. For I believe that God longs to touch each of us with healing compassion, so that we can live with freedom in his kingdom.

SOME WORDS ABOUT
JOURNALING

*J*ournaling questions have been included after each chapter in this book. You are invited to reflect on the ways each story and their explanations relate to your life.

I can testify that journaling is a highly effective tool in the spiritual life. It should be undertaken with a relaxed attitude; we need not create works of art in our writing; we should strive to better understand ourselves and our God. As Eddie Ensley and Robert Herrmann state in their book *Writing to Be Whole*: "Through the time-tested practice of spiritual journaling, you will have the opportunity to look at your past and your present and take the whole of your life to a merciful God for healing. You can explore your spirituality, work on mending your relationships, and begin to see the world from a new perspective."

By all means, give yourself the gift of good supplies. You may want a large journal that opens flat to give you the space to really express yourself. Purchase good pens that don't skip or blotch. I enjoy using colored pens and pencils to sketch or express feelings in color.

If at all possible, set aside a special time during the day to read and journal. For some people, an early-morning time works well. Others go to the park with a sandwich during their lunch hour. For others, there is time for their own inner work after the children have been tucked into bed.

Write freely, and don't edit at all when you write. You may want to wait days or weeks before you reexplore your writing. I hope you enjoy an exciting time of self-discovery. Some journal keepers leave blank pages after their entries so that they can later respond to what they have written.

Your journal is confidential and no one else will read it. It is inappropriate for even a priest or spiritual director to read another person's journal.

I have found that on about the third page of journaling a lot of truth and deep feelings begin to emerge. If possible, give yourself the gift of journaling at length. In the future, you may want to join a prayer or discussion group at which you can share your journaling safely. The value of support in the spiritual journey cannot be overestimated.

Blessings on your work.

Lyn Holley Doucet

IGNATIUS:

THE UNLIKELY SAINT

Then someone wrestled with [Jacob] until daybreak. . . . Jacob named the place Peniel, "Because I have seen God face to face," he said, "and have survived." The sun rose as he passed Peniel, limping from his hip.

GENESIS 32:25, 31–32

Vanity. Temper. Stubbornness and pride. Vice—and a propensity for trouble. Are these the makings of a saint? Perhaps we should not be discouraged about our own failings when we look at the life of St. Ignatius of Loyola.

He was born in 1491, near the French and Spanish border, into a family of Basque nobility. He was baptized Iñigo de Oñaz y Loyola. His family was controversial and had been in trouble with the king at one time for opposing his reign. The king reduced the size of their estate, but they survived and their fortunes were restored. Iñigo was the youngest of thirteen children.

The Basque people were well known for their stubbornness, fiery courage, and impulsiveness. Some writers assert that Iñigo was spoiled, but perhaps he was in equal part emotionally neglected. His mother may have died giving him birth or soon after. A brooding and confused spirit developed in a part of Iñigo's heart, but he usually kept this well hidden.

Iñigo was probably a handsome boy with thick blond hair who adopted the sophisticated grooming and colorful dress of his era and class. When he was a teenager, he was sent to live with relatives, the powerful Velázquez de Cuellar family. He lived as royalty, spending time in the court of King Ferdinand becoming accustomed to damask sheets, silver services, and the attention of servants. Iñigo's development of courtly manners gave him a lifelong refinement of speech and manner. He spent his spare time in wild revelry and seeking the companionship of the fairer sex. He got into serious trouble with the law during an Easter vacation to his home and escaped imprisonment only because he was supposed to be a tonsured cleric: one who is destined for the priesthood. There was little evidence to support this claim, but probably because of his powerful family connections, he was not punished.

After the death of King Ferdinand, the Velázquez family fell out of favor, and Iñigo was forced to become a soldier. This was a major turning point of his life.

Go with me now, back to a pivotal day in the life of this saint-in-the-making. It is the spring of 1521, and French troops have entered the Spanish town of Pamplona. The town itself seems ready to welcome them, as the Spanish cause appears hopeless. In fact, certain officials of the Spanish court and some of the leading townspeople have hammered out an agreement with the French to end the siege peacefully. Proud Iñigo de Loyola cannot accept this however, even after a meeting with French and Spanish negotiators. Iñigo returns to the fortress portion of Pamplona Castle to wage what has been described as "a most lopsided and absurd war." With only tattered remnants of the Spanish force carrying on the battle, death is everywhere, and Iñigo thinks he will die. He confesses his sins to a fellow soldier, an accepted practice of the day.

He is gravely wounded, but it would seem that God is not finished with him yet. Iñigo returns to his childhood home to be nursed back to health.

Iñigo was still vain; he endured a painful surgery that reshaped his leg so that he could once again wear the knee-length pants that were fashionable. Despite surgeries, or because of them, from this time forward Iñigo walked with a slight limp. Perhaps, like Jacob of the Old Testament, who fought with God's angel, Iñigo was marked by the One who created him. He had begun to wrestle with God, and God had great plans for him.

As he slowly and painfully recovered his health at Loyola, nursed by his sister-in-law Magdelena, Iñigo asked for reading materials. He wanted to read tales of war and chivalry. In this pious household, however, there were two books available: one about the life of Christ, the other a book about the saints. Iñigo would read and daydream. Sometimes he daydreamed about performing heroic deeds of chivalry and winning the heart of a noble lady. When he did so, he was initially joyful. Later, however, the joy faded, and he was left with bitter depression. Then he would read of the lives of St. Francis or St. Dominic, and he wanted to be just as they had been: giving all for God. The joy that came from these musings was deep and lasting. He began to understand his own heart and the workings of God there. This was the germinal work in his discernment of spirits (read further about this topic on page xxiii). He also began to be remorseful for his many sins. He began to be converted.

Still the courtier at heart, when he rose from his sickbed, Iñigo traveled to Montserrat, where he kept a knight's vigil before the

Black Madonna, laying his sword and shield at her feet. He then journeyed to Manresa, where he was to spend a year being a "fool for Christ," practicing harsh penances and eating little while living in a cave. The women of the town took pity on him and helped him. Some were to remain lifelong friends. At Manresa he despaired. He was filled with self-hatred and he could not understand the love of God. He thought that God could not love him because of his many sins—Iñigo even contemplated suicide. But God kept breaking through to the troubled mind of this confused knight.

Beside the River Cardoner, God reached out to Iñigo in a powerful and lasting way. God touched him in mercy and love and taught him as a schoolmaster teaches a little child. Perhaps the motherless child in the hidden recesses of Iñigo's lion-sized heart was beginning to be touched and healed.

Iñigo set out to educate himself in the classics in Spain and France. He begged for alms and went without food, and yet he began to reach out to others in love and concern. He developed in full his Spiritual Exercises, a set of gospel-based, contemplative practices, his stunning gift to the world and especially the church. He was always in prayer. He signed his name Ignatius for the first time upon his graduation with a master of arts degree in Paris, because he so admired Ignatius of Antioch. Just as Jacob of the Old Testament became Israel, this wounded and complex man Iñigo marked his change of heart with a new name. He had seen God.

Ignatius gathered his comrades again for a different war, the war for souls. He attracted two friends who were destined for sainthood: Francis Xavier and Pierre Fabre. Trouble often dogged his footsteps, however. He was constantly speaking to people about spiritual things, and the Inquisition questioned him and imprisoned him several times. He was told what to say, what to wear, and to whom he could speak. This must have been a bitter pill for this still-proud man! But his life was sustained by the One who touched him by the River Cardoner, the One who longs to touch us all.

Ignatius's life was marked by contrast: illness and energy, wealth and poverty, pride and debasement, lasting joy that replaced despair. His *Spiritual Diary* is filled with his tears and his ecstasy. His life took its final form in Rome, where he served the poor with great personal hardship and founded the Society of Jesus, that group of amazing and educated men known as Jesuits. He and his comrades had to abandon their plan of living and working in the Holy Land, and it was with great pain that Ignatius released this dream. The pope blessed their Society in 1540. Ignatius labored on, serving as Superior and writing the Society's constitutions. He died in Rome in 1556.

What can this man of contrasts mean to us today? He seems somewhat bigger than life, and yet he is just like we are in so many ways. He sought his place in this world amid confusion and doubt. He cherished his friends, who sometimes disappointed him. He made a lot of mistakes. He loved well and poorly; he was wise and mistaken; he was moody and steadfast. The truth is that God got hold of Ignatius and wouldn't let him go. And so it is with us, ordinary men and women of a different time and place. God's love never changes.

To Be Freed from Fear

It is characteristic of the good spirit to stir up courage and strength, consolations, tears, inspirations, and tranquility. He makes things easier and eliminates all obstacles, so that the person may move forward doing good.
IGNATIUS OF LOYOLA, *The Spiritual Exercises*

A part of you was left behind very early in your life. The part that never felt completely received. It is full of fears.
HENRI J. M. NOUWEN, *The Inner Voice of Love*

I met Abbigail in the patio of the building where she worked. The day was perfect, clear, and cool, and we sighed with pleasure as we settled at the picnic table and unpacked our Piggly Wiggly salads and Diet Cokes. I had known Abbigail for many years as a church friend, but we rarely had a chance to talk on a personal level. I knew that her recent mission trip to Haiti had been wonderfully healing for her, but I really didn't know why, or how these changes had taken place in her.

"I had never realized fully the insecure way in which I had grown up and the wounds that had been left," she said. "My parents are good and loving people, but we had hard times. Mom's hurtful past resulted in controlling and dominating behaviors. My father was ill a lot. Doctors told him he wouldn't live a long life due to a serious illness. Subconsciously, I feared I'd lose him, and poor Mom would be left with five children to raise. I developed unconscious fears of loss and abandonment."

At eleven years old, Abbigail felt she had been in "a time of darkness." Her maternal grandmother and beloved first cousin passed away, and her little brother hurt himself badly and fell into a coma. There was so much suffering. One day she heard her mother say, "I just can't take it anymore. I'm just going to run away."

"On some level," said Abbigail, "with all the sadness and stress, I thought that Mom, the one person I knew loved me, really would just give up and leave. But I know she was doing her best." She stopped speaking, and the dappled sunlight accented her soulful face. "I love and respect both of my parents very much. They are good people. They, too, were victims of their own childhood hurts. Their faith in God sustained them through their trials, and they passed that eternal gift on to me."

Abbigail went on to say that as a middle child she often felt invisible, especially passed over by her stressed and busy father. As the years passed and she became a young teenager, very traumatic events happened with other people that caused her to be fearful. Her brother drank heavily, and she learned to distance herself emotionally from most people she knew. All of these events formed a dark chasm of fear in her heart. But her feelings remained unconscious. While in her teens, she continued to enjoy an active social life and to date and go to parties.

"It is only recently that I have realized I fear so many things," she said. "I had so much trouble developing trust—trust of myself, others, and God. It affected my whole life and all my relationships. I didn't feel lovable and worthy, either. I couldn't feel God's unconditional love."

Often our perception of the love of God is determined by the love of our fathers. "Dad and I talked about my perception of our relationship. He was devastated at the thought that I didn't feel his love. Today, at every possible time, he tells me how much he loves me, and I know without a shadow of a doubt how very much I am loved."

Abbigail looked sad as she picked at her salad. I felt guilty for bringing all this up for her. More than that, I felt the penetrating sense of her pain. Writing this book has not been easy; I am charged again and again with walking with others in their pain. In many ways it is my pain, too.

Though her spirit carried its many wounds, Abbigail clung to her faith. She attended Mass every Sunday and often during the week. She prayed often as her husband and children flourished in her care.

In her forties, she began to live with a growing sense that God would use her for mission work. An opportunity arose when good friends were going to travel to Haiti on a Catholic mission trip. The group's preparation began long before the plane left the airport. One of the missionaries, Katherine, worked with them to prepare their hearts. She talked with them about humility, in putting easily hurt feelings aside. "Develop a servant's heart," she said. They were instructed to receive the sacrament of reconciliation, pray often, and receive the Eucharist. Another leader spoke to them about healing and deliverance. He taught about forgiveness of self and others and how the "enemy" tries to come against Christians and make them people of fear. He instructed them to renounce the enemy with the authority of Jesus Christ. As the group made their preparations, the situation in Haiti became turbulent. Abbigail wondered about the advisability of her trip, yet she felt undeniably called to go. She spent more time in prayer.

As the preparations proceeded, Abbigail became enveloped in a series of coincidences that she believed were sent by God's hand. At the last minute, she needed additional money to buy extra supplies for the mission. Relatives, not knowing of her difficulty, were prompted to give her just the amount she needed. As she boarded the plane, her heart was filled with fear. She strapped herself in and got out her daily devotional book. The reading for that very day was Julian of Norwich: "All will be well. All manner of things will be well." Abbigail smiled and relaxed.

Abbigail had to walk through extreme fear when the plane dropped them off at a remote Haitian village. The jeep that would take them to the mission was not there. Their plane left them and roared back into the sky. Remains of burned tires on the bridges and in the streets were evidence of recent riots. There were only three missionaries: Abbigail and her friends, a husband and wife. The three stood in an open field in the rain, waiting. Soon they were surrounded by puzzled villagers, who encroached on them more and more. The missionaries had been warned not to make eye contact. Abbigail and Justine, the woman standing beside Abbigail, raised their hands and began to sing praise songs. Covered with dripping rain, they sang and sang. As she raised her voice and lifted her eyes to the sky, Abbigail realized that she was staring fear in the face. And she was surviving. As Abbigail and the others sang, a rainbow began to fill the sky. As her fear grew, the colors of the rainbow intensified. "It was my sign," she told me.

Suddenly, a man pushed his way through the crowd to stand close beside them. Turning to the sullen villagers he explained, "I know these people. They are good people. They have come to help us."

Abbigail will never forget the warm and welcoming smile on the man's face. She calls him "our angel." The same man was scheduled to be married at the mission church that week. The group praised God that he was nearby and had come to their aid. The villagers relaxed and withdrew.

Once their ride arrived and they traveled the bumpy miles to the mission, the mission group's work really began. They presented hand-sewn suits to the many women who would be married during the group's stay. The women were overwhelmed with the wedding suits; even the simple slips and underwear were objects of wonder to them. Abbigail prayed with each woman.

Before leaving the United States, Abbigail and others had collected hundreds of pairs of shoes. These were distributed to the delighted, barefoot people, young and old. In every simple and grateful face, Abbigail saw Jesus.

In her bunk that night she read the day's devotional in her little book. It said, "Jesus is very pleased with the hospitality you have shown him. His heart is moved by it." Even as Abbigail drifted into an exhausted, peaceful sleep, she could sense healing in her soul.

In the powerful healing and deliverance services that were conducted during her stay, Abbigail felt her own heart being renewed more and more. She had felt the loving and providential care of God all during her trip, and even before. The unconditional love of God the Father was warming her entire being. She was filled with true forgiveness and love.

Abbigail paused in her retelling of this story. Her eyes met mine. She related that while on the trip a deacon in one of the communities had given her a cross made of special wood and a "missionary Bible." "It wasn't just any cross; it was his cross. It was given with the stipulation that I pray for him. Can you imagine? He asked me to pray for him?"

"Of course, I can imagine it," I said. "You have a light within you. Don't you see it, Abbigail?"

She could not reply at first, overcome with emotion. "God is so good," she said.

Abbigail had lived much of her life encased in the pain of her childhood. She had functioned well in the world, and yet she knew that all was not as it should be. As she took steps in faith to overcome her fears, she was guided by God's good spirit. She discovered in her life a lasting joy. A lasting healing. As she says today, "God is so good."

As Ignatius lay ill in his childhood home, he began to devise his system for discernment of spirits. He noted that when he meditated on things of the world, such as performing great deeds of chivalry, he felt happy at first. Later though, the aftertaste of such thoughts was a bitter depression. As he pondered becoming like the saints he read about, especially St. Dominic and St. Francis, he felt joyful and remained so. Ignatius felt that these latter thoughts were led by the good spirits, expressed as thoughts of God, love, and service.

Most of us can testify, as Ignatius did, that many of the things we thought would make us happy had only a temporary effect. As we look around the world, we see many in search of wealth, power, and recognition. These don't seem to be the truly happy people. On the other hand, those who work for others and for God, such as the late Mother Teresa, seem to have a deep-felt sense of lasting joy. Through our service to others this joy enters our hearts.

For Journaling and Reflection

❊ Are there wounds in your life that cause you to place an emotional distance between yourself and others? If so, write about how God could help to heal some of these issues.

❊ Are there issues in your life about which you have considered counseling? If you have not sought counseling, what has delayed you?

❊ What specific steps could you take to overcome fears in your life?

❊ How do the good spirits work in your life? What things of God give you lasting joy?

2

A Healing after Divorce

I will call back into my memory the gifts I have received . . .
stirred to profound gratitude. . . . I will consider how all good
things and gifts descend from above . . . just as the rays come
down from the sun, or the rains from their source.

IGNATIUS OF LOYOLA, *The Spiritual Exercises*

*R*ebecca sat in the prayer meeting, uncharacteristically silent. Usually a cheerful and talkative person, she was slumped in an attitude of quiet despair. *Too much has happened,* she thought. *Too much has happened.*

It was hard for her not to be jealous now as she looked around at the other women in the group, most of them happily married and with secure incomes and futures. *I was like that not so very long ago.*

Her physician husband, Mack, had been pulled into court during a malpractice suit. During the prolonged legal battle, Mack had started coming home later and later in the evenings. Soon the news was out among their friends: Mack was having an affair. He quickly asked for a divorce. Rebecca was shocked and devastated. She tried to get him to attend counseling in an effort to save their twenty-year marriage, but he refused.

Rebecca shook her head and focused on the present moment. The leader of the prayer circle was asking for petitions. Rebecca wanted to pray, but her request turned into angry words. "He's telling me now that we never had a good marriage, can you imagine? Twenty years and four children and now he discovers this?" Her voice shook. Her friends offered comforting and sympathetic words.

Oh, this doesn't help, she thought. *I just keep saying the same things over and over. I really hate being this angry, bitter person. When will this pain lessen? I want my life back!*

Rebecca tried to bury herself in her work as a Catholic-school youth director, but even her students noticed that she wasn't the same. Her days passed in dreary progression as she longed for the past. Months went by as she struggled with leaving her beautiful home and moving into an apartment. She was now living on her own with her two younger children.

Soon it was time to plan the school's annual mission trip, deep in the mountains of northern Mexico. Rebecca had always loved this trip. Now she was unmotivated and depressed as she made the travel plans for herself, other sponsors, and the group of students. They would spend a week repairing the homes of indigenous people in the area and participating in Mass and meals with them.

The group arrived at the dusty mountain village and was welcomed by its residents, who came out of their small, plastered homes to embrace the group with joy. They praised God that their friends from the United States had returned to them. These warm and cheerful people had always impressed Rebecca in the past, but now she saw these Christians in a new light.

These people are so happy with what they have, she thought. *I had forgotten how joyful they are with so little.* Her thoughts rested on her own situation. *Yes, I have lost much; I can't pretend otherwise. I have lost my life's companion and the vision of what my future would be. Yet I must remember, I still have so much.*

The week of hard work and prayer passed quickly, with festive group meals and liturgies filled with song and punctuated by drums and the strum of guitars. Even the poorest families dressed their children for Mass with shined shoes, immaculate clothes, and ribbons in the girls' hair. Watching the beautiful children, Rebecca felt a humble yet profound softening of her bruised and hardened heart.

One morning she greeted the sunrise as she sat high on a rock above the steep valley floor. Birds sang as streams of gold, pink, and apricot light suffused the rocks and plants around her. She felt her anger and pain easing, and she felt a new emotion, gratitude, which had been long absent.

"God," she prayed, "no one could see this beauty and doubt your presence. The wonderful people in this village struggle so much, yet they have you. They have a joy that I want to know again. They have a faith that puts mine to shame. Forgive me, Lord, for all my angers, my self-pity. Let me see what I still have—and what you are still pouring out for me."

The tears that came then were gentle and healing tears of gratitude. Rebecca thought of her children and of a grandchild on the way. She thought of her work, which would never make her rich but would allow her to live in a simple and fulfilling way. She praised God for her strong body and her many good friends. She began to accept her life with all of its changes, and she slowly began to say, "Thank you, God."

It was a changed and healed Rebecca who sat at another Theresian prayer meeting months after her initial experience there, when she had felt so angry and bitter. She knew that her anger had been understandable and that she had needed to express it, that it had been a step on her healing journey. Now she was in a new place. When the leader asked for prayers from the group, Rebecca said simply, "I pray in thanksgiving for all my many blessings."

To St. Ignatius, everything was a gift. This humble saint never felt that he deserved anything. In fact, he was sometimes amazed that God was good to him at all. He was touched that God did not want to punish the world but wanted to shower humanity with good gifts. In his worldview, all came from God and all returned to God. Ignatius gave himself completely to God's will, in which he found the higher gifts, the things that did not decay or fade away. In the above quote from "Contemplation to Gain Love," Ignatius leads us to love as God loves, without condition. Despite persecution Ignatius forgave others.

It is easy to become bitter when others hurt us or when our dreams are crushed. This is a very human response, and these feelings come to most of us. But like Rebecca, we can allow our hearts to be touched by the beauty of the world and all of God's goodness. We can humbly begin to forgive others and experience healing as we realize that all is a gift.

For Journaling and Reflection

❧ How do you handle disappointment? (Be honest!) How can expectations sometimes become burdens?

❧ Most of us have experienced a betrayal or another type of hardship. Can you journal about this aspect of your life? What helps you recover from such hurt?

❧ Describe any experience you have had with gratitude.

❧ Describe any part of your life (home, work, church) that is in transition. Write about these changes.

3

Give the Body What It Needs

[T]he Lord does not require you to do anything exhausting or harmful to your person. He wants you to live taking joy in him and granting the body whatever it needs. . . . Attend to your bodily necessities for his sake.

IGNATIUS OF LOYOLA, IN A LETTER TO AGNES PASCUAL

*S*heri Roger sat outside the medical clinic, her head in her hands.

"Why is my life coming apart, Lord? I have tried so hard to be good—even perfect! I have tried so hard."

Sheri had just been examined by her internist. The doctor had looked at her and said sadly, "Sheri, if your weight doesn't increase soon, I am going to have to hospitalize you. Your organ systems could shut down. For the next three weeks, I want you to see this nutritionist twice a week." The doctor handed Sheri a business card. He paused. He didn't have to say, "This is your last chance." Sheri understood.

A devout Catholic, teacher for disabled students, and mother of two, Sheri had struggled with anorexia for seven years. She saw herself as fat and disgusting, though she was a mere eighty-five pounds spread over a fragile five-foot-three frame.

She sat in the car and recalled a recent visit with her therapist. She loved her psychologist, and he had tried so hard to help her. Toward the end of their last session, he had looked at her intently and said, "Sheri, I think you loathe and hate yourself. I can't understand why, but you need to understand why. I think that there is something in your past that has hurt you deeply that you haven't fully explored. It has inflamed this self-hatred. If we can bring this to light, I believe you can get well."

Sheri knew what that "something in the past" was, though she had tried diligently to suppress it. Sheri had mentioned to her therapist that she had become pregnant her freshman year of college while she was dating the man who was now her husband. They had tried to make things right. It had not been easy, but they had married, helped each other through school, and even welcomed another child. However, there was something Sheri hadn't told anyone—not even her husband.

On the night that she'd confessed to her parents that she was pregnant, her normally mild-mannered father, whom she adored, had changed before her very eyes. Blind with rage, he had hurled obscenities and ugly names at her. A part of Sheri died that day, and that part had never been brought back to life.

After the confrontation with her father, she had gone on with her life and resumed her relationship with her parents as though nothing important had happened. But now, as she sat in her rain-swept car outside the doctor's office, she faced some hard facts.

Her body knew about that night. Her heart knew. Her therapist had said that she was punishing herself by starving her body. But what could she do? She had tried to move on and be okay. She had tried to eat normally like everyone else, but her willpower wasn't working. Food repulsed her and obsessed her at the same time. Did an evil inner voice constantly tell her that she didn't deserve to eat? Didn't deserve to live? Now as the wet wind blew against her parked car, she prayed harder than she ever had.

"Lord, my children need me. My husband needs me. I'm dying! What can I do? How can I possibly get well?"

In the stillness the answer came: "Talk to your father."

The idea filled Sheri with such fear that she trembled. What if he said those ugly things again? What if he still felt that way about her? She and her father had maintained a careful, polite emotional distance since that fateful night.

"I can talk to my mother, Lord," she said. "Not him. Oh, not him."

She slowly drove to her parents' home. She sat in their carport, trying to control her breathing. She got out and entered the kitchen, only to meet the worried eyes of her mother. As usual, her mother offered her something to eat and asked about her doctor's visit.

"Mom, I'm so sick!" Sheri's iron will was beginning to weaken. She began to cry. "I know what's wrong, Mom."

"What?" Her mother put her arms around Sheri. "What is wrong?"

"It's that night, Mom. When I told him about the baby. Those things he said. I was always his little girl, his princess. Oh my God, how could he . . . ?"

Her mother's voice was quiet. "Why don't you ask him?"

Sheri turned to find her father standing with them in the kitchen. With shock she realized that tears were streaming down his face, too.

"I'm so sorry, Sheri," he said. "I should have never said those things. I was so hurt. All our wonderful plans for you in dust, but that's no excuse. All these years I have regretted it, but I guess my pride or my fear wouldn't let me talk to you. It was evil what I did. And you've done so well. I'm so proud of you."

They hugged and cried together.

After this, Sheri didn't get well all at once. She slowly made her way back to health with the help of her therapist, internist, and nutritionist, and with continued prayer. She still struggles with her body image. Sheri says that she is relearning how to be a person of dignity and worth. But in the dark place in her heart where the destructive forces of anger and self-hatred thrived, a deep spirit of consolation and forgiveness has flowed in. It has brought forgiveness for her father—and for herself.

When Ignatius began his conversion, he tortured his body with whips, rough clothing, fasts, and exposure to the harsh elements. Like Sheri, he struggled with self-hatred. As he grew wiser in his walk, he realized that the body is given to us to help us serve God. He began to counsel others to care for the body, realizing that he had compromised his own health by some of his practices. What Ignatius did in zeal and guilt, Sheri did in blindness, self-hatred, and guilt. Her motives remained hidden to her until her prayers released a secret. During her greatest agony, God moved in a powerful way to restore Sheri's body and mind.

For Journaling and Reflection

❧ Write about your relationship with your parents or other people who raised you. How have these relationships been filled with peace or conflict, sorrow or joy?

❧ Are there actions by your parents or other authority figures in your life that you want or need to forgive? If so, write about this and bring it to prayer.

❧ How do you care for your body? Do you provide all its necessities, or are do you abuse it with bad habits or addictions? If so, consider why this is the case. Bring this to prayer and write it out. (Never hesitate to seek help from physicians or counselors, as Sheri did.)

4

Please Heal My Inner Heart

Take, Lord, and receive all my liberty, my memory, my under-standing, and all my will—all that I have and possess. You, Lord, have given all that to me. I now give it back to you, O Lord. All of it is yours. Dispose of it according to your will. Give me your love and your grace, for that is enough for me.

IGNATIUS OF LOYOLA, *The Spiritual Exercises*

Laura McCauley sat, frightened, on the examining table in her doctor's office. The fifty-five-year-old grandmother had always enjoyed wonderful health. She had some inner scars—but doesn't everyone? Her childhood had not been the best, she sometimes told others. But that was far behind her now. She had a happy marriage and much to live for. But at this moment, her doctor was acting a little too concerned about her test results.

"You have a serious narrowing of some of the vessels of your heart," he said. "I don't think it is a fat obstruction; it appears to be a genetic trait that has caught up with you at your age. I will put you on some medications, but I must tell you, this is serious. I think surgery would be a last resort."

Laura left the office in a daze and went home to discuss the doctor's information with her husband. They also needed to decide if they would proceed with a scheduled trip to New Mexico.

"Yes, let's go," said her husband. "Remember, this trip includes going to Chimayo to the healing chapel."

Only days later Laura found herself on her knees in the quaint El Santuario del Chimayo, which has been called the Lourdes of America. The chapel is a combination of Spanish and Native American flavor, filled with folk art and surrounded by the crutches and notes of thanks left by people who have been healed there. She prayed hard, but she didn't have any special feelings. She returned to her motel, and her husband took a walk while she rested. But she couldn't rest. She found herself again on her knees, in the cool ceramic bathroom of her motel.

"God," she asked. "Did you bring me here to heal me?"

Suddenly a startling insight came to her: There were many ways in which her heart needed healing!

"Oh, Lord," she continued, "most of all, heal my inner heart. I surrender my life to your will. Just let me know that you are with me."

The tears began, and soon her body shook with sobbing. A vision as clear as reality drifted into her consciousness. She saw herself as a little girl of eight, standing on her aunt's porch. She had been sent to this aunt to live for a whole year when her mother had become ill. She realized in one moment, on her knees in a bathroom, how traumatized she had been by this displacement.

"Oh, God, it wasn't my mother's fault! I forgive her. I give these memories to you. Don't let me hold on to bitterness! I surrender all to you, Lord. Make your forgiving will my own."

At that moment, Laura felt her heart being healed. A warm light seemed to fill her chest. Her crying continued but quieted down. Later she was exhausted and slept for many hours.

Back at home, Laura visited her doctor. He shook his head in confusion. "I can't believe it, but the blood in your vessels is flowing much better. I am going to cut your medicine in half."

Laura smiled and gave thanks—for improved physical health, but mostly for the healing of her "inner heart."

Laura had found the surrender to God's will that St. Ignatius always extolled. This great saint believed that we have nothing to fear in abandoning ourselves to one who loves us more than we love ourselves. If we realize, as Ignatius did, that all life is a gift, then we can learn to stop clinging to our own expectations of how our lives *should* be. When this happens, we are free to realize, as Laura did, that God desires all that is best for us and gifts us still.

For Journaling and Reflection

❧ Take some time to examine your "inner heart" today. Do you sometimes cling to past hurts and bitterness? What steps can you take to let go of what is hurting you?

❧ Write about any physical symptoms that are causing problems for you. Try to imagine what good could come out of either the symptoms or your process of dealing with them.

❧ If appropriate, spend some time writing about your frustrations and about the possibilities in your life, despite any physical problems.

❧ How do you feel about surrendering all to God? Does it make you feel fearful? If so, why? Do you have an image of God as harsh and punishing?

❧ Does the idea of surrender make you joyful? In your journal, explore all these feelings about God and surrender.

5

Tasha's Story of Good and Evil

It is characteristic of the evil spirit to cause gnawing anxiety, to sadden, to set up obstacles.

IGNATIUS OF LOYOLA, *The Spiritual Exercises*

The fact is that we do not comprehend the greater mysteries nor find the larger insights without passing through the pathos and suffering of life.

JOHN SANFORD, *Mystical Christianity*

Tasha was a young, rather frail, Danish woman in her twenties when she met Momed. He was older than she and was a handsome, charismatic man from Morocco, deeply immersed in the Muslim faith. Tasha fell in love with Momed, with his charisma, his kindness, and his strength. She longed to have the faith that he did, his inner assurance that everything was going to be all right.

After a few months, Momed and Tasha traveled together to Morocco to live. Momed was a Muslim counterpart to what

Christians would consider a preacher. Each day many people came to his home to hear him speak. He daily gave away most of what he had, and he seldom knew where his next meal was coming from. The words *Allah will provide* had a true and present meaning for him. He helped the poor and ill in any way that he could, and he seemed to live without worry or fear.

Tasha tried very hard to be just as Momed was. Almost from her first day in Morocco she battled illnesses of many types. Her stomach was often upset, and she was frequently feverish and weak. The only relief that she received was from the women of the community who worked as herbalists. Still, Tasha persevered in Morocco, trying to embrace Momed's God, and she followed strictly all the tenets of his religion. She felt that in this way she could be strong and have faith as he did.

Her situation got steadily worse, however. She became unable to sleep and had vivid nightmares. Finally, she saw a doctor who gave her medication to help her sleep, along with other medications for her ailments.

Tasha was experiencing debilitating stress from her illnesses, and she was burdened with a dark sense of evil and doom. At this time, she began to be overwhelmed by "hearing" the thoughts of others. She heard these thoughts, and she was accurate in what she heard, as later events proved. She said, "I had a deep sense of being overwhelmed by all the emotions and thoughts of others. I was on sensory overload, and I didn't know what to do. I tried to stay by myself, but I could do this only so much in that culture." She was rapidly approaching a breakdown.

Things came to a climax one warm afternoon in an open-air restaurant where Tasha frequently went with Momed and his friends. As she entered the restaurant and sat down, she was bombarded by the thoughts of those in the place. Thoughts and feelings whirled over her like waves over the sand. She trembled as she reached the crisis. She was about to lose herself in a serious breakdown.

At this moment, she heard a voice "as big as the universe" say to her, "Tasha, lie down." She was filled with this voice, and she started to leave her chair and lie on the floor. Then, in a flash of understanding, she knew that the voice was saying, "Tasha, surrender."

At that moment, she let go of all the voices and thoughts, all the illness that racked her body. When I spoke to her about writing down her story, she said, "I want you to make clear the difference between the moment before the voice spoke and the moment after. All became peace and love. All was different. The voices stopped. My suffering just stopped."

She began to understand that she was called to surrender a life that was terribly wrong for her. She had tried to follow all the tenets of the Muslim faith and to make her home in a country far from everything she had known.

Her dilemma stemmed from following a person rather than looking within, listening to God's voice, and finding her own path. She still believes that Momed is a good person and that his religion is life-giving to his community. She believes that the problem was that she was walking a path that God had not chosen for her. She was trying to be someone else and to earn the love of God that she already possessed. She says that the voice that said, "Surrender," was saying, "Surrender to my chosen path for you. Surrender to my love. Stop working at religion and submit yourself to my care."

When I later met with Tasha, I was surprised to learn that she remained in Morocco for two more years after this incident. She was no longer ill, and her heart and mind were turning slowly back to her homeland. Tasha sadly said good-bye to Momed, and she was not to see him again. Once back in Denmark, she returned to her true love of music and gained entrance to a music institute there. She developed a deep spirituality that was based on love and compassion for herself as well as for others. She lives simply, with few possessions and many friends.

I can testify that Tasha has bloomed in the new garden she has created for herself. She practices her spirituality daily, and she gives love and care to others in a gentle way. Her health is good, and she daily strives to eat well, to exercise, and to be at peace.

When Tasha came to Louisiana to study Cajun music twenty years ago, I met her and made a true friend. She has received rewards for her music, but more important, she knows that she is traveling the path that God intended for her. She no longer tries to be someone else.

Twice in his life, Ignatius determined to stay and work in the Holy Land: once at the beginning of his conversion, and once when he was working with his companions, those who would be Jesuits, to find a mission. Each time this dream was thwarted by circumstances. Despite Ignatius's amazing strength of will, he had to accept God's will instead. This was difficult for him, and yet he trusted that there was a path of service for his God that was his own. And indeed there was! He began his work in Rome with his companions, and the effects of his work spread all over the world.

There is a Hasidic proverb that reads, "When you get to heaven you will not be asked why you were not more like Abraham and Jacob. You will be asked why you were not more fully yourself." Dare we believe that God has a plan for each of us? Dare we have the courage to seek God's voice and his direction? As Tasha discovered, trying to walk another's path can lead to destruction. We can be enticed by the promise of an easy ride on the coattails of another person. This is especially destructive when the path leads us away from God's will for our lives. Tasha's healing meant embracing who she was, embracing God's love and care for her that was already fully present.

For Journaling and Reflection

❀ What do you believe about people and their callings and destinies? If you believe that God actually calls each person to a special path, how does a person discern that path? If you can, describe a particular "calling" God has for your life.

❀ If the mind and spirit are present in every cell of the body, how can physical illness in your life be related to your emotional and spiritual health? How has this synergism (the relationship of the physical and the spiritual) been reflected in your life?

❀ How could you become misdirected and choose the wrong path? Write about this.

✤ Has it been easy or difficult for you to remain faithful to your chosen path? Explain, and examine this aspect of your life.

6

Talking with Roberta about Breast Cancer

The person must be free enough to be himself before the Lord, to look at the Lord, to receive from the Lord, to commit himself to the Lord, to grieve with the Lord, to let himself be consoled by Him. The more freely and expansively he enters into these stages, the more deeply he is likely to experience them.
WILLIAM J. CONNOLLY, S.J., *Notes on the Spiritual Exercises*

*M*y friend Sharon O'Neill and I donned our earphones in the little broadcasting room. Our role as radio broadcasters was new to us; this was our fourth show on Radio Maria, a Catholic broadcasting station.

We were joined by a friend of Sharon's, Roberta, who was battling breast cancer. After our opening prayer, Sharon turned to Roberta and began a discussion of how faith had enabled her friend to have peace as she dealt with the diagnosis and underwent treatment.

"I will never forget the day of the diagnosis," said Roberta, a trim lady of fifty or so. "My husband and I stood in the parking lot of the medical center. The sun was shining, and people were walking about as though nothing had happened." She smiled, but the strain showed in her eyes. "My life had changed. I was in deep shock. My husband held me and said, 'How do people get through things like this without faith?'"

Roberta is a dancer, and she stretched gracefully in her chair, holding a book entitled *All Things Bright and Beautiful*. She read a selection from the book called "Surrender." The author wrote about ancient wounded and gnarled grapevines in an Italian village; the weathered vines yielded the brightest blooms and the juiciest, richest grapes.

"This is what God does with our wounds," Roberta said. "God brings forth from them the greatest gifts. I have found so many new friends as we cancer survivors support one another. I cherish friends and family so much. I have compassion and empathy that I didn't possess before this happened."

The discussion moved on to chemotherapy and Roberta's hair loss, which she called "the biggie" for women. "I knew it was coming, and so I went out and brought a red wig, a black wig, and a blonde wig. I said, 'Let's see if we can have fun with this.'"

She said that all her hair finally came off in the shower one day, and as she walked out with her body wrapped in a towel, her husband said, "Well, it doesn't look so bad."

"He has been my constant support. He calls me his little baby blackbird." Roberta laughed as she told stories about the red wig she had ordered. It was "way more red" than it was supposed to be, and she tried to dye it with Rit fabric dye. (Hair dye wouldn't work since the wig was synthetic.) Then she tried a brown marker, and then shoe polish. The three of us were laughing at the saga of the red wig, and I thought, *I didn't expect this conversation to be so easy. What a joyful, courageous lady.*

"I am one of the fortunate ones," she said. "I have had love and support, and most of the treatments have not made me ill. But there is no right way to do cancer. You do what you can. You feel what you feel. It looks like they caught this in time, but I will live under a cloud for a while. My children will worry for a while. My daughter wonders if she will get breast cancer later. My son has a friend whose mother died of this, so I guess it has been hardest on him."

She looked down and pondered for a moment. "I just say, 'Your life is in God's hands, trust him,' when the children ask me questions. Yes, we think that all will be well, but it is so important to live every day—day by day, moment by moment. Well, I guess that sounds a little trite."

My mind flashed back to that morning, when I had walked out to feed my dogs. The sun had lit the dawn sky with pinks and yellows, and the breeze had blown softly against my face. I had sadly remembered all those who had just lost their lives to terrorism (the terrorist attacks on the Pentagon and World Trade Center were quite recent then), and I thought, *I am alive. This is the greatest gift, just to be alive and feel the wind on my face.*

I smiled at Roberta as the show's closing music began. "No, Roberta, it doesn't sound trite at all."

"Surrendering ourselves into God's care." These are poetic words that are very hard to put into practice. Roberta and her husband discovered this path as they faced cancer together—the cancer that would change their family's life forever. Roberta feels that God is healing her, yet she has also found the fruits of suffering, the gifts of her wounds.

Ignatius was no stranger to illness and suffering. In fact, during his conversion he suffered almost any pain and deprivation one could name. Yet he never lost his faith or his zeal for the work he felt God had chosen for him. He had chronic stomach pain for most of his life, and sometimes he rose from a sickbed to visit others who were also distressed. In his great compassion, he fed and sheltered the poor and ill, knowing exactly their feelings, their pain. He always counseled his friends to abandon themselves to God's care. Be pure of heart, he believed, and all will be well.

For Journaling and Reflection

❀ Are you or is someone close to you suffering from cancer or another life-threatening illness? If so, how have you dealt with the suffering? How have you tried to make sense of it—or have you not tried to make sense of it yet?

❀ What situations, if any, are beyond your own fixing? How could you abandon these situations to God's care?

❀ What, if any, positive things have come from the challenges in your life?

❀ In what ways do the gifts of life, such as good relationships, ease our sufferings?

❀ How much do you enjoy humor? How could you explore this area of enjoyment more fully?

❀ Do you tend to be a person of worry, or does trust come somewhat easily to you? Explain.

7

Healing Our Vices

[T]he name of Jesus imprinted itself so intensely within me and I was so fortified or seemingly confirmed for the future that tears and sobs came upon me with a new force. . . . [M]otions of copious grace and devotion continued to help me, along with peaceful, continual tears. . . . I now perceived that [confirmation] was being presented to me in the name of Jesus . . . immediately I moved forward into confession with humility and many tears.

Ignatius of Loyola, *The Spiritual Diary*

*M*argaret has gorgeous red hair and a finely structured face. Her eyes filled with concentration as she practiced the vocal exercises that we had just begun at our voice retreat.

"This is hard," she said, "and I feel very vulnerable when I sing before the group. But I have to remember that it's a miracle I am singing at all."

She looked at me, and her eyes shone. "Did you know that I used to smoke three packs of cigarettes a day? I didn't want to quit. I loved to smoke."

Margaret continued to share with me that much in her life was out of control during those years. She had felt like an efficient zombie: shut down, just going through the motions.

"There was so much from my past that I refused to deal with. You see, I smoked my emotions. That way I didn't have to think about them; I just smoked them away."

Margaret's life hit a low point, and she felt her defense mechanisms loosening their hold. She began meeting with a counselor, and she grieved intensely as she slowly dealt with her scars.

"But most important," she said, "at this time in my life I accepted Jesus as my Lord and Savior. You know, this is not just for Protestants to do." She smiled. "I had been my own Lord. I was so proud of the way I could handle everything—until I couldn't."

One day soon after her conversion experience, Margaret was driving in her car, her heart filled with the continuing struggle to heal fully. "Lord," she said to the empty car, "tell me what you want me to do. What are you calling me to?"

After her plea, Margaret clearly heard the voice of the Lord: "Margaret, I want you to quit smoking."

She was stunned. This had not been what she was expecting at all! She was expecting to be called into some form of exciting service to God.

"I said, 'Maybe I can go to India and work with Mother Teresa. Lord, you have got to be kidding about quitting smoking! I can't!'"

Again the voice came, clearly and audibly, "Margaret, I want you to quit smoking."

"Okay, Lord, but I can't do it. You have to do it in me." The emotions of that moment returned to Margaret's face as she looked at me now. "I began to sob so intensely that I had to pull my car into a parking lot. I thought my heart was breaking, but it was really mending. I put down my cigarettes, and I never desired them again. The craving left me totally that day.

"The person that the Lord wanted me to love and serve that day was me," she said. "I guess I had never fully known that I was worth loving, worth saving. And he desired to save not just my physical body but my spirit and soul as well. As I said earlier, while I was smoking, if I felt an uncomfortable emotion, I just lit up. The smoke was truly a screen for everything. But it never solved a thing. My Lord and Savior saved me that day." She wiped a single tear from her face. We went back to our vocal exercises, and I admired Margaret's high, clear voice in a new way.

For St. Ignatius, Jesus was a clear and ever present person. Jesus was truly his Lord and Savior. In reading the saint's works, we note that he felt reverence but not separation between himself and God. As St. Ignatius's faith grew over the years, he began to desire more Christ's will for his life, and to desire nothing but that. In the saint's later years, God was as close to him as his own breath.

At the same time, St. Ignatius considered himself only an unworthy servant. Yet his faith and the ongoing revelation in his heart gave him the confidence to believe that God truly spoke to him, that God greatly desired his salvation through Jesus Christ. This confidence infused his Christian service with his gifts that we still experience today.

William Barry, S.J. tells us that "God creates the world in order to invite each one of us into a relationship of intimacy, friendship or mutuality. If this is true, then God is always making overtures to each of us, is always communicating with each of us" ("Does God Communicate with Me?" *America*, 3 December 2001).

Margaret heard God's voice as she drove her car on an average day. We should listen for his voice! The voice of God is trying to break through.

For Journaling and Reflection

❧ How do you react to the expression "I have accepted Jesus as my personal Lord and Savior?" (There is no right or wrong answer to this question.)

❧ Have you had a personal experience of deliverance or healing in which you felt the clear intervention of God? If so, write about it.

❧ What habits in your life may interfere with your living freely in God's joy? What kind of prayer might you offer to God concerning these habits, or what help could you seek?

8

The Loving Arms

The lover gives and shares with the beloved what he possesses, or something of that which he has or is able to give. The same Lord desires to give me even his very self.

IGNATIUS OF LOYOLA, *The Spiritual Exercises*

*L*ife had long been a struggle for Virginia. Her husband had left her for another woman after ten years of marriage. She was left to raise three small boys. To make ends meet, Virginia worked at a plastics factory, punching out forms, a job that was ordinarily assigned to men. She says today, "I worked mostly around men. I heard a lot of comments that weren't very nice. But this job paid more than any other I could get, and so I stuck it out."

Virginia had always dreamed of being a nurse. However, she had married very young and had happily expected to be a home-maker and mother for many years. That dream, too, had ended. Now she wondered if it was time to look at her old dreams. She didn't get a lot of encouragement. She was given many reasons why she couldn't possibly complete the schooling needed.

No one in her circle of family and friends tried to help her figure out how she could accomplish her goal.

Virginia says today, "It took my grandmother, old and frail, to put her arm around me and say, 'Ginger, when are you gonna go be a nurse like you're supposed to?' "

Virginia made her plans. She worked during the day and went to nursing school at night. She struggled to put the needs of her children first, taking them to their ball games and helping with homework and projects. Because of this, her grades suffered. She was traumatized the day she stood in the dean's office and the dean advised her to drop nursing. "You are never going to pass these next three courses," said the dean. "There are a lot of other things you could do."

Virginia went home to think and pray. She was a deeply spiritual person. She had already come through many adversities with God's help. Now she felt that God was telling her quite clearly, "You can do it. Proceed as you planned."

She returned to the dean and said, "God is going to help me through this."

In an aggravated manner, the dean scrawled a sarcastic note on Virginia's folder: "Virginia thinks that God is going to get her through these courses." Virginia was even more wounded, yet she was still determined.

Struggling through academic probation and pressured to make the necessary grades, Virginia finally completed her courses and became a registered nurse. At her pinning ceremony she sang in her rich and beautiful voice, "To God Be the Glory."

Excited and gratified, Virginia began work. She was assigned to the emergency/preoperational section of the hospital. The work was stressful and the hours were long, but Virginia reveled in it. She was bringing solace to suffering people, something that she had longed to do. She was receiving respect and making good friends among the nursing staff. Virginia was proud of being part of her profession.

Incredibly, just when her ceaseless work and prayers had made her dreams come true, the unthinkable happened. While she was driving home from work one cold, drizzly winter evening, she was hit head-on by a drunk driver. An ambulance quickly returned her to the hospital she had just left. Doctors and nurses worked frantically to save her life. She had suffered innumerable broken bones, a collapsed lung, and of most concern, severe head injuries. A team of doctors removed a blood clot from her brain. A plastic surgeon did preliminary repairs to her crushed sinus cavities and nose so that she could breathe. Tension was high, and Virginia's situation was touch and go.

For Virginia, the most amazing part of the story was still to come. Two days later she awoke in the hospital's intensive care unit. As her eyes opened, she struggled to realize where she was and why she was there. Then she had the most wonderful experience.

"As I lay helpless in my bed, I clearly felt loving arms around me. They were living arms, warm and with substance. These arms encircled and held me tenderly. For many minutes I felt the love that emanated from these arms. They were the arms of Christ."

As Virginia lay exulting in the comfort of the enfolding arms, she heard an inner voice say, *Virginia, it is going to be all right. I am with you. You are going to recover.*

It was not easy. Her recovery was long and painful, yet Virginia was filled with peace. She stayed many weeks in the hospital and received physical therapy for a year after her release. In addition, she had to have reconstructive surgery several times on her face.

Virginia shows few visible signs of her injuries today, although she laughs and says that her nose is cuter now. There are faint scars on her face, but they are visible only up close. She worries a little that she will experience arthritis in some of the many break points that have now healed on her body.

The supervising nurse questioned Virginia thoroughly and intensely when she wanted to return to work after more than a year of recovery. Concerned about the head injuries, the woman asked, "Are you sure you remember things? Maybe you should take disability."

"Yes, I remember things." replied Virginia stoutly. "I didn't work so hard to become a nurse to let anything stop me now!"

Now when she tells the story, she smiles. "What the evil one meant for harm, God meant for good. I cannot tell you the blessings that have flowed forth from this accident. First and foremost, I understand what it is to be in pain and helpless. My compassion and patience have increased greatly." She chuckles, "Every doctor and every nurse should spend time in a hospital bed. It's the best place to learn a lot that we need to know."

I met Virginia recently at a retreat in the beautiful town of Grand Coteau. I was her retreat director, but she was the one who taught me so much. It was humbling for me to encounter such courage and perseverance in adversity. As we talked, Virginia and I found that we shared a love of singing. She hadn't sung much since her accident. Now she spoke to me about her desire to take voice lessons and rediscover her singing voice.

"You know, I have a vision. It is night at the hospital. I am making my rounds, and I am singing softly. The sound floats into each room. And the patients feel safe—and that they are wrapped in loving arms."

Perhaps more than most of us, St. Ignatius felt the loving arms of Christ around him. He battled with his fears of sin and punishment, yet the love of God kept breaking through to his troubled mind. He embraced the beloved "who gives himself to me."

For Journaling and Reflection

❧ Write about any accident or illness in your life that required or still requires healing.

❧ What specific aspects of your body or soul do you need to bring to God for healing?

❧ What is your reaction to Virginia's story?

❧ Write about any time in your life when you have felt a particular closeness to God.

9

Healing after the Ultimate Loss

I have many grounds and indications to assure me that she [our sister in Christ] is now in the other life, full of glory forever and ever.

IGNATIUS OF LOYOLA, IN A LETTER TO TERESA REJADELL

*M*y friend Sharon O'Neill and I continued to grow in wisdom through our new show on Radio Maria. But I was dreading our interview on this particular day. As a doting mother, the subject hit too close to my heart: surviving the death of a child.

Phoebe Hebert, the woman who bravely consented to the interview, is a dignified woman. She appeared calm before the program began, and Sharon and I talked with her about various questions we might ask, questions about the tragic death of her young daughter.

When the program began, I asked Phoebe to tell us about her daughter, Ashley, who was twenty years old when these events began to unfold.

A smile lit Phoebe's tender face. "It may sound like a cliché, but Ashley really did light up a room when she entered. She was blonde and very pretty. She loved to act and was in dramatic productions. She was humorous and lighthearted. Her favorite statement to me was 'Lighten up, Mom! Life's too short!' "

Phoebe paused, smiled, and adjusted her earphones. I could tell that she was enjoying these memories. My chest was tight, and I was feeling a little light-headed. Phoebe, however, seemed fine.

Phoebe then told us that one evening her twenty-year-old daughter did not come home from her usual date with her long-time boyfriend, Kevin. Phoebe didn't panic right away. She thought that maybe Ashley had spent the night at a friend's house and had forgotten to call. However, the next day there was no news of Ashley. Even worse, Kevin's car was found parked near a dance club, with Ashley's purse still inside.

Phoebe paused and shifted in her chair. Her eyes were sad. "I knew Ashley wouldn't have gone far without her purse."

"Phoebe," I said, "Can you share what you were feeling at this time?"

"Fear. So much fear. Yet, I tried to carry on. There was nothing I could really do. We were all praying. People across the country were praying. I was still hoping that this was some youthful indiscretion that would turn out okay. It wasn't."

As the police became involved, the story unfolded. A young man about Kevin's age was heavily involved in drugs and drug trafficking. He had somehow gotten the idea that Kevin was a narcotics officer. (He wasn't.) This young man ran into Ashley and Kevin at the dance club and invited them to take a ride to Lake Martin, a nearby, secluded area. Since they were acquainted with him, they consented. There in the woods he shot them, execution style.

"This guy wanted to show off for the big dealers. And he was using drugs heavily. Ashley was just at the wrong place at the wrong time," said Phoebe.

It was time for the short break in our show. I was filled with sadness. But Phoebe was all right. I hugged her and thanked her for being so brave. When we were on the air again, I asked Phoebe what had helped her to heal. She said, "I feel that things happen for a reason. And I feel that Ashley is in a better place. She's safe; she is at peace.

"I have a significant other in my life. His name is Allen. And he has been a rock. And so many friends came forward to help. You should allow people to help you when something like this happens. Let people come close."

"What are some of the things that people said that were not helpful?" I asked.

"Well, things like, 'God took her.' Or, 'Well, you have two other daughters, you'll be okay.' Or, 'It's time to get over this and move on.' But, I didn't really take offense. Some people can't look at your pain. It's their own stuff they're dealing with."

"What helped the most?"

"The presence of people. The hours of listening that my friends gave me, helping with chores. God's amazing grace. And talking about Ashley. Don't pretend that a deceased person never existed. That hurts the most."

As the conversation continued, we discovered that Phoebe had years of hardship to face, as the young man who killed her daughter and Kevin went to trial. Sharon asked, "How did you feel in that courtroom, Phoebe?"

"Angry. Very, very angry. But it's funny. As time passed, I began to have sympathy for the young man's parents, especially his mother. She was going through such a valley of suffering and loss. And I have worked with drug-affected young people. I know that they do things on drugs they would never do otherwise. At first, I wanted the death penalty, but, you know, he's in prison for life. That's not a good place to be. His parents are dealing with this for life. It is all too sad to stay angry about. Sometimes the anger returns; all these feelings return. But they become softened, and you can live with them.

"I had to discover things that fed my soul. Singing at my church is very nourishing for me. And dancing. I dance sometimes at workshops or conventions.

"You can survive the death of a child. And you can flourish. It's not what you want, but you have to get busy living or get busy dying. I decided to live. I'll always miss her. But I feel that she is all right. And she would want me to be all right, too."

How often we avoid thinking about death because of our fear and dread. Yet at the heart of our struggle is our hope in the risen Christ, who leads the way to eternal life. This is the hope that has helped to heal Phoebe's heart after the loss of her daughter. It is this assurance that gave Ignatius his profound consolation when he considered death.

For many parents, our own death is easier to consider than the death of a child. Despite Phoebe's testimony, each time I visit this story, my own heart recoils in fear of loss. Yet many parents survive the death of their children. Some of them, like Phoebe, learn not just to survive but also to flourish.

Phoebe says that it is very important to understand that each person grieves differently. There is no right time frame or way in which to grieve. One heals as one can. We can only offer to the one who grieves love, time, and a listening ear. This is especially true if we ourselves are in grief. If you are grieving now, I pray that exploring your darkness through this book will be a help to you at this time.

For Journaling and Reflection

❄ Have you suffered the death of someone close to you? If so, what, if anything, has helped your healing?

❄ Try to write about a person you have lost. What qualities did he or she have that were especially meaningful to you?

❄ Is it easy or difficult for you to believe in eternal life? What helps you? What are your stumbling blocks?

❄ What feelings did you have as you read Phoebe's story? Do you think you would have reacted as she did? Why or why not?

10

The Healing
That Really Happens

May Our Lady intercede between us poor sinners and her Son and Lord; may she obtain for us the grace that, with the cooperation of our own toil and effort, our weak and sorry spirits may be made strong and joyful in his praise.

IGNATIUS OF LOYOLA, IN A LETTER TO AGNES PASCUAL

Our bulldog, Beau, and our son's pug, Bruno, (our "grandchild" we are baby-sitting) have decided to wrestle under my chair as I type. They keep knocking against my feet until I am forced to stop and remove Bruno to the outside. I laugh at their aliveness, their plump beauty. Beau came into our lives not too long after we lost another dear bulldog, Toby. He has truly filled a space in our hearts with his sweet, undemanding presence, which is healing for my husband, Dee, and me.

It is so important not to deny the healing that happens in our lives. And sometimes we do deny it, through intellectualism, overrationalization, or even false humility, such as saying, "Why would God bother with me?" Author Tricia McCary Rhodes refutes these excuses in her book, *The Soul at Rest*. She states, "God wants to meet your deepest needs. He wants you to see, know, taste, and experience him in ways that shake you to your core. He longs for you far more than you could ever long for him. He stands ready to reveal himself, enfold you in love, speak to you with power and touch you with grace."

The characters who people this book have been touched by that grace. Most of them said to me, "I don't tell this to many people," while glancing surreptitiously around the room. At times, our interviews took on the feeling of espionage: What if others really knew? Would they think that I am crazy or a religious fanatic? But by the end of the story, their eyes always were lit from within and they whispered, "It really did happen! God touched me!" This leads me to believe that many healing stories are lost because, out of fear, we hold back our praise of God.

Perhaps we sit at the feet of Jesus' mother Mary, as St. Ignatius did, asking her to intercede for us, to move us to the healing we desire. After all, as a mother she understands and can help us be strong and joyful, even when healing does not seem to come in the ways we have prayed for. In Mary we find the model of sober grace, developed through adversity and coupled with gratitude for God's gifts in her life. We are called to participate with her and all Christians in the paschal mystery, the large and small cycles of dying and rising in our lives.

For Journaling and Reflection

❧ Think about your work with this book. What insights, if any, have you gained about God's healing?

❧ Many of us have some resistance to healing because it often requires a fundamental change in our lives. Write about your own resistance as you best understand it, or your lack of resistance.

PRAYER TO THE GOD
WHO HEALS

I trust that you are healing my life, God.
In hope I receive your grace.
In peace I will sleep.
In peace I will rise.
Let me savor your gifts in each day.

Send streams of water to restore me, God,
Refreshing my heart in hidden places.
I thirst for your touch in every moment,
I surrender my life to your care.

11

Mysticism in the Mountains

As he sat by the river [Cardoner], the eyes of his understanding began to be opened; not that he saw any vision, but he understood and learnt many things, both spiritual matters and matters of faith and of scholarship, and this with so great an enlightenment that everything seemed new to him.

IGNATIUS OF LOYOLA, *The Autobiography*

I was spending time in the Sangre de Cristo Mountains completing a retreat with the writer Paula D'Arcy. The second-to-last day of the retreat was devoted to a "vision quest," during which the spiritual seeker goes into the mountains alone to fast and seek direction in his or her life.

Throughout the week I had made numerous remarks about my lack of a sense of direction. I decided that for me to hike into the mountains alone was not a good idea. Still, I felt a little ashamed as other, more rugged pilgrims planned their routes, polished their hiking boots, and searched out their sacred places.

Finally, I talked to a fellow retreatant, Kaye, who has an immune deficiency disorder. A typical vision quest would not work for her either. So, with a third woman, someone who often visited the mountains, we took a car trip to Chimayo, the healing chapel described in chapter 4.

The magic of the trip began as we drove through the mountains, listening to inspiring music on the tape deck. By prior agreement, there was no talking among us, so our minds and hearts were free from distractions as the car wound over the mountain roads. Each selection on the tape seemed to perfectly match what I was feeling as I began my vision quest. Our four days of preparation had allowed me to be focused in the present moment and open to the gifts of only that moment. It is a way of living that I seldom practice, as my mind (like most people's) is often reliving the past and anticipating the future.

We entered the little village of Chimayo, and our friend dropped us off. We entered the quaint stucco church, with its folk-art statues and the tossed-aside crutches of other pilgrims. In one area, notes were stuck to the wall thanking God for specific healings.

As we entered, we saw people setting up for Mass. I became so excited, but I chuckled to myself, *Oh, so excited about Mass? What's gotten into you?* My friend and I sat near the front as the cheerful, elderly priest greeted worshippers, speaking in both Spanish and English. He looked right at us and said, "We begin today by remembering that God loves us. God loves you!" He shook his hands emphatically toward us, repeating, "God loves you!" and we smiled and nodded. As the liturgy continued, I seemed to be in a mystical place, surrounded by a sort of light, a sense of safety and peace. Everyone and everything seemed beautiful beyond words.

My friend planned to stay in the cool of the church and pray, but I wanted my vision quest to have some taste of the wilderness, so I left to visit the nearby stream. As I walked, I could hear falling water in the distance, and I followed the sound. Soon I was traveling through someone's yard. I fully expected to be turned away, but the two men in the yard just smiled at me. Then I saw it: my sacred place!

The clear, cold water tumbled over a man-made wier, splashing and sparkling down. Lacy green willow trees and yellow-blooming plants embraced the soft grass of the bank. I could walk right up to the edge of the water and sit comfortably. I observed as yellow and orange leaves fell into the waterfall and floated like little sunlit rafts in the stream beyond. A flock of gray-and-white pigeons flew high, then swooped over my head. Had I searched for many days, I could not have found a more beautiful place for my vision quest.

I sat in stillness, thanking God for the gift of this place. Suddenly, I felt a great oneness with all I beheld. I was in the splashing water. I *was* the splashing water, the flowing water, the cool filtered sunlight, and the trees. Buddhists believe that at our death we may return to matter; perhaps we become leaves or drops of water. At that very moment, this idea of the persistence of matter seemed a good thing, and nothing to fear. I shook my head and smiled; I had a hope that my soul would be saved into the "beatific vision," as St. Ignatius might have called it, or "heaven." For me, at that moment, this oneness I felt was a taste of that heaven.

As I sat in my sacred place, I experienced, as Ignatius wrote about in the *Spiritual Diary,* "a greatly increased, quiet, and tranquil devotion, along with tears and some insights." I saw for a few moments that I had nothing to fear and everything to rejoice for. Healed within me, at least for a while, were the loneliness and alienation that I sometimes felt—that feeling of being alone in the crowd. In this unity with my surroundings, I was fully healed and fully whole. I desired and needed nothing more.

Long after I had this experience, and weeks after I had written about it, I studied Ignatius's experience in Manresa on the banks of the Cardoner River. There Ignatius felt more knowledge than sixty years of study would have brought him. His mind was infused with wisdom and insight that would help to sustain him all his years.

I was embarrassed! I had no intention of comparing myself to this great saint. Maybe people would even think that I had made this experience up in order to be like him. Oh, dear! Yet it is cowardly to deny the workings of good in one's life. The experience did happen to me, and it is one of the reasons I have the courage to write and to share my heart so freely.

St. Ignatius lived through war, epidemic disease, and rampant violence. He thought several times that he would die of illness before the morning and made his last confession. There was little that was certain in much of his life other than his faith, with which he faced each day with calmness and joy. His greatest fear was that in sin and blindness he would disappoint the Father, the Son, and the Spirit and that he would become lost.

Today we enjoy vastly improved amenities and conditions, yet our confidence is sorely shaken when we are attacked and as we go to war or participate in others' wars. And, perhaps, we should examine other ways in which we become lost. Do we value money and possessions above all things? Do we work so many hours a week that we lose touch with family and faith? Perhaps we are critical, projecting all of our fears and weaknesses onto others, or we let anger turn into hate. These are but some ways we become lost and far away from Christ.

As I sat beside the water in Chimayo, I discovered a secret that Ignatius knew. Let this moment, the one you are now living, fill you. It will teach you so much. Let your gratitude for life, for God, fill your heart with love and save your soul.

For Journaling and Reflection

🌿 Write about an experience that has been a spiritual high point for you.

🌿 Some people get lost in fear, anger, or overwork. What form does being lost take in your life? Write about how you might better find yourself when situations are difficult.

🌿 When are you filled with tranquillity? What practices, if any, lead you to tranquillity?

🌿 What effects do natural surroundings have on your joy and faith? If being in nature is helpful, how might you create more opportunities to go there?

12

I Was an Invisible Child

I will consider how God dwells in creatures; in the elements, giving them existence; in the plants, giving them life; in the animals, giving them sensation; in human beings, giving them intelligence; and finally, how in this way he dwells also in myself, giving me existence, life, sensation, and intelligence; and even further, making me his temple. . . . I will consider how God labors and works for me in all the creatures on the face of the earth.

IGNATIUS OF LOYOLA, *The Spiritual Exercises*

Your true identity is as a child of God.

HENRI J. M. NOUWEN, *The Inner Voice of Love*

*T*here were ten of us seated around my Oriental rug as the holy candles flickered softly on my table. The Michael the Archangel candle glowed red with passion as we spoke of our early years.

The question was: What were you like as a child of eight or so? Many had shared that they played with paper dolls, dressed up the dog, swam in Louisiana coulees, and worried when their parents fought. Now the group looked toward Renee, who clutched her journal with tense hands. "I quit my last journaling group when this kind of question came up," she said. "But I told myself that with God's help, I would do it this time."

"You don't have to answer, Renee," I said. "Keep it between you and God, if you wish."

"No, I will. I have a special reason to answer tonight," said Renee, a grandmother with light brown hair and a kind face. "I felt invisible as a child. I was the sixth of seven children. My father was a sharecropper, and he drank and ran around. My mama was into survival. I often thought, *It would be a long, long time before anyone would miss me if I disappeared.*" There was a silence in the room. Another woman nodded in recognition.

"But I have realized something!" Renee said unexpectedly, giving us a big smile. "We had to walk back a long way from school. Mama was supposed to pick us up, but Daddy would never let her. So, I took my time, and I went to the library. Do you remember those old stereoscopes, the black and white ones?" We nodded.

"Well, I can remember now, like it was yesterday. I would put in pictures of lions or zebras, or a plaza in Paris, and I would look for hours. I would think about all the places I could go where I might be seen; where I wouldn't be invisible. And it would make me happy. Then, I would get books on all those places, lots of books, and after I walked home I would go into the closet and read and read and read. I would go to these wonderful places."

The candles on the table richly glowed against the wildflowers I had placed in a small vase. The silence in the room was rich with shared thoughts, empathy, and love.

Now Renee was radiant. "I never realized until I wrote about this that I had some things worth remembering. God was there! God was there in that library. I had a childhood after all."

We can only speculate about many things in St. Ignatius's childhood. It is probable that he lost his mother when he was very young and that this left a hole in his heart. Many children of nobility of that day were very attached to their wet nurses and made provisions for them in their wills. The young Ignatius had a nurse of this sort, but it is not known how close they were. When he was a teenager, he was "given as a son" to another family. It is reported that he went to live with them willingly and in high spirits, but one must wonder what he was really feeling. How could you leave all that was familiar? How could you be given away? How could you say good-bye to a childhood in one place and try to be someone else's son in another?

Ignatius did experience much luxury in his early life, but there also was much turmoil. His circumstances changed with the political winds, and he must have experienced fear and insecurity at a relatively young age. But when we read *The Spiritual Exercises* we realize that for the converted Ignatius there was no circumstance in his life that was not of God, unless it was sin that Ignatius chose for himself. He saw God as laboring for humanity as God made himself known in the trees, the animals, and the heart of each person. For Ignatius, God was always there, always merciful, and always just. Although he spoke and wrote little of his childhood, I believe he would say, "God was there. Yes, God was there in my childhood."

For Journaling and Reflection

❧ What were the most trying circumstances of your childhood?

❧ In what ways was God present in your childhood?

❧ When you were a child, what was your relationship with the outdoors? What is that relationship like now?

❧ When you were a child, was there a special place or a particular activity that was a real retreat for you? Can you revisit a similar place or activity now?

13

The Death of Rose's Father

*For he sees and knows what is best for you; knowing all things,
he points out the path for you. And in order for us to discover
this path with the help of his grace it is very helpful . . . to travel
along the path which it becomes clearest to you is the most
blessed . . . with ourselves being embraced and made one with
these most holy gifts.*

IGNATIUS OF LOYOLA, IN A PERSONAL LETTER

*R*ose weighs about ninety-five pounds and is barely five feet
tall. Her small size, however, is more than compensated
for by her amazing energy; she rarely seems to tire.

Rose and I lead musical ensembles at our church. We were fortunate enough to go to Minnesota for a weeklong workshop
with Jeanne Cotter, a well-known musician and vocal teacher.
Rose had carefully chosen the song she wanted to perfect that
week: "Now We Are One," which is often sung at weddings.
"This song goes to an F," she said, "and that's a little out of my
range. I have to sing it at weddings, and I want to sound better."

Once we arrived at the conference, however, Jeanne put Rose to work on the "Pie Jesu," a haunting song that tells of Jesus' passion. Day after day, Rose struggled with this piece, because it was pitched very high, indeed. The strains of "Pie Jesu" echoed throughout the halls of the simple retreat house, and I coached her as best I could, using notes I had taken when Jeanne taught. Rose rarely complained, but she wondered aloud a few times about why she was learning this song and what had happened to the work she had planned to do on "Now We Are One." Jeanne did not waiver in her choice for Rose, however. "This has the range that I want Rose to work on."

The retreat ended, and we returned home to Louisiana. A friend from the retreat, Carl, sent Rose the sheet music for "Pie Jesu" as a surprise gift. After we had been home about a week, I received an e-mail from a mutual friend of Rose's and mine that Rose's father had died suddenly the night before. I phoned Rose, and she was barely able to speak through her tears. She told me that her father had not been seriously ill and that no one had expected his death. Traumatically, her father had died at Rose's home, while she and her husband struggled to perform CPR and call for emergency help.

Rose sobbed into the phone, "I said, 'Oh, God, don't let him die now. Not here and now.' But I think he was gone before the ambulance even arrived."

The next day Rose and I talked by phone again. Now her voice was firm, and she said, "I have made a decision. I am not going to let fear stop me. I am going to sing the 'Pie Jesu' at my father's funeral. I have the sheet music now; Carl sent it to me." I gasped a little at her courage. She continued, "I need you there in the choir loft with me. I just need to see your face as I sing, just as I did in Minnesota." She paused, then said, "As I began to plan this funeral Mass, my heart began to mend. Back at the retreat, I surely did wonder why I was learning that song. Now I know that God had a plan."

The music at Rose's father's funeral was outstanding; many of her musician friends came to help with the liturgy. At the close of communion, my courageous friend pulled herself up to her full five feet and began the "Pie Jesu" in honor of her father. Her high, clear voice echoed throughout the cathedral. A sense of holy sadness pierced all our hearts. On Rose's face, sorrow mixed with joyful peace.

I knelt nearby in the choir loft and sent all my strength to her. Even as I write this, the rich emotion of that day returns—and I see God directing our path even before we know the way we are to take.

When Ignatius was younger, he saw harsh penance as a primary way to save his soul. As he grew wiser, however, he discouraged such practices, saying instead that in our prayers and meditations we can be given great gifts, gifts beyond those induced by artificial suffering. He named these gifts "intensity of faith, of hope, of charity; spiritual joy and repose, tears, intense consolation; elevation of mind, divine impression and illuminations. . . ."

These gifts are available to us today if we choose to travel along the path that is most blessed. Ignatius counseled his friends that God would order their paths if they surrendered to his divine love. For Rose, this surrender involved trusting her teacher at the vocal clinic and overcoming her fear and grief in order to sing. Without her full cooperation with the Spirit, Rose could not have reaped the spiritual fruits that were waiting for her, all the while giving God the glory.

For Journaling and Reflection

✿ Describe in your journal any grief that is affecting you at this time in your life.

✿ Is it difficult for you to follow the prompting of the Spirit? Can you remember times you have done this?

✿ Do you believe that God has special gifts waiting for you? Why or why not? What might those gifts be?

14

The Power of Suffering Love

*[The enemy]refrains from telling us about the great comfort
and consolation which our Lord is accustomed to give to such
souls when the new servant of the Lord breaks through all
these obstacles and chooses to suffer along with his Creator
and Lord.*

IGNATIUS OF LOYOLA, IN A PERSONAL LETTER

I arrived at the Bourgeois family home at nine in the morning, as I did every Tuesday and Thursday. I sat for a moment, fighting the feelings of inadequacy that dampened my spirits each time I visited this home.

As a special education teacher for hospital-and homebound students, I was at the Bourgeois home to work with Jean-Paul, the family's eldest son.

Jean-Paul had porcelain skin, luminous green eyes, and black, silky hair. In those beautiful eyes, however, there was little that spoke of understanding or even recognition. Jean-Paul's development had not yet reached that of a one-year-old, but he was then ten. He was not toilet trained and had almost no oral language skills.

Jean-Paul's mother greeted me at the door and offered me coffee or a cookie, but I was determined to get to work. I was attempting to teach Jean-Paul commands in sign language. For six weeks, we had been working on *come* and *sit*. I would set up two chairs and work with Jean-Paul, getting him to move from one to another and sit in the designated chair. We had made a little progress, and I hoped that if Jean-Paul could learn sign language, he could communicate more easily with his family.

As it usually happened in my work, I had become attached to both Jean-Paul and his parents. I often talked at length with his parents about their son and the whole situation. But things steadily got worse with Jean-Paul. Over the months I worked with him, he began to abuse his face with his fists. This happens with these children sometimes; no one really knows why. I arranged for two psychologists and the district nurse to evaluate Jean-Paul, but no one had any answers.

One day I arrived to find Jean-Paul's mother in tears. Her son's chin was a mass of lacerations; the family was considering tying his hands so that he could not hurt himself. I tried hard to control my own emotions as I viewed this beautiful boy. His father had stayed home from work to help us that morning.

"Let's talk," I said. We got Jean-Paul busy with a few toys and sat down. His mother paused periodically to stop Jean-Paul from hitting his chin.

I was one of many people who knew the history of the Bourgeois family. Jean-Paul's father had been a Catholic priest who left the priesthood many years earlier. After he had been a layperson for several years, he met Sarah and they married. In a year, Jean-Paul was born.

In the small town where the Bourgeois family lived, it was reported that certain senior women in the community felt that God was punishing Robert for leaving the priesthood—by allowing his son to be born severely retarded. Of course, such talk made me furious. It was the perfect way to add insult to injury, not to mention the false and hateful picture it painted of God.

Now I said, "I'm in over my head here. I wonder if the stress of my teaching Jean-Paul is causing some of this." His father answered, "Well, you teach so gently, and with rewards. The psychologist said that's not it—but we can't find any answers."

As Jean-Paul played quietly, our conversation drifted to the suffering that the family experienced. "How do you handle this?" I asked. "Can you explain it in any way, based on your faith?"

Jean-Paul's father, slight with salt-and-pepper hair, looked at his wife and smiled. "Well, I don't think that God is punishing us, although those thoughts surely crossed my mind. It was just so odd the way the whole thing happened. You know, I have preached so many sermons on suffering. I urged my parishioners to join their suffering to the cross, to suffer with Christ for the redemption of the world."

He paused, sipping his coffee, and shook his head, "But when it happens to you, you start all over. You don't know anything. Nothing makes sense. You just learn, day by day, to go on. To try your best, to pray for nothing but strength."

Jean-Paul did not get better. The day came when I accompanied the family to a home for the disabled, where Jean-Paul could receive daily medication and staff members could help prevent his self-abuse. Jean-Paul had the look of an abandoned puppy when we left. I paused at the gates and felt as though my heart were coming out of my chest. I could barely drive home. I could not imagine what the Bourgeois family was feeling.

Many years have passed now. The family had five more children, an act of courage in itself. I ran into one of their grown daughters the other day. She reported that Jean-Paul's self-abuse had stopped, but little else has changed. He adjusted well to the home. He likes the food there. "Mom and Dad are doing great," she said.

I learned humility from this experience. I learned through the Bourgeoises' example to embrace a God of mystery without bitterness. I learned once again that everything would not be explained on this side of heaven. I learned about the healing power of suffering love.

Early in his Christian walk, Ignatius realized that life itself brings enough suffering for the Christian without adding too much more. In his letters, at this time, he offered sympathy to his friends who had problems, and he urged them to throw themselves on God's mercy. He also encouraged them to give their bodies enough food and rest, and to give their minds solace so they could continue in the Lord's service. Ignatius could not fully explain suffering, but his faith gave him hope that all things were working together for good in the divine plan. He offered the hope of the Lord's consolation. Through his example, we can realize that when outside circumstances do not change, our hearts can heal.

For Journaling and Reflection

❀ What circumstances, large or small, in your life cause ongoing suffering or problems?

❀ Describe ways in which you have been able to experience God's consolation in the midst of problems.

❀ Is it easy or difficult for you to emulate the faith of the Bourgeois family? Explain why.

❀ How can we give real help to those around us who are in difficulty?

15

Allowing God to Sustain the Creative Life

[T]he enemy comes with his third weapon. This is a false humility. When he sees how good and humble the Lord's servant is . . . the enemy then injects the suggestion that, if the person adverts to anything that God our Lord has given him by way of deeds or resolves and desire, he sins through another species of vainglory because he speaks approvingly of himself.

IGNATIUS OF LOYOLA, IN A PERSONAL LETTER

I sat at my signing table at the Jefferson Street Market and watched as couples, groups of women, and families filtered through the doors. Occasionally I would sign a book, but I wasn't really that busy. It was not a great night for book sales. I focused on being in the moment and enjoying the sights and sounds of Lafayette's "Artistwalk." The groups that I watched had traveled around to various galleries and boutiques, viewing the work of the artists there. There was a sort of magic in the air, a festive feeling—the week's work over, a time to relax and just *be*.

As I stood up and stretched, a woman's eye caught mine. She rushed up to hug me. "Do you remember me? I was in your Artist's Way class. I'm Michelle."

"I do remember you," I replied. "Wow! When was that? Five years ago?"

We chatted for a moment and then Michelle looked at me, her eyes filled with excitement. "You won't believe how my life has changed since that class!" She opened her purse and produced a beautiful brochure entitled, "Ceramics and Mosaics by Michelle."

"I'm doing it; I am claiming my creative gifts. I have pieces in several of the galleries here, and I am full up on commissions."

"Well, Michelle, you have certainly made my night. I am so proud of you. You overcame those negative voices, huh?"

"I did! It was so hard. You know how it is. Every time I sat down to work they would start: 'Who do you think you are? How dare you think you are talented? People are going to laugh at this stuff.'" She sighed. "But I just said, as we practiced, 'Thank you for sharing, now go away!' You have to do that a lot, but it finally starts working. I am not going back now!"

As I deepened my study of St. Ignatius, I was struck by his portrayal of the evil voices. They were so like the negative voices described in Julia Cameron's book *The Artist's Way*. These vicious inner voices conspire to tell us that we never do anything right. They try to convince us that we have no talent and nothing to give to God or the world.

As we look around our beautiful world, we see the God of creativity. This God did not content himself with creating one pink flower; he created thousands. He created not one lizard, but hundreds of types of lizards; not one cookie-cutter person, but billions of unique souls. Truly, God delights in variety, in creativity, in creation. And God delights when we create. This I believe with all my heart. As Ignatius said, "These desires [to serve] do not come from yourself, but are given to you by the Lord." God calls us to be cocreators in the world that has already begun.

The evil one will tell us over and over that we have nothing to offer. We can easily lead colorless lives of safety and depression if we allow these voices to overcome us. As Ignatius told Teresa Rejadell, "He draws you away from greater service and from our own greater peace of mind."

St. Paul tells us that we are many parts of one body. Yes, some will travel across the seas to help others. Some will preach; some will speak in tongues to heal. Some will find a way to teach a struggling child to read; others will draw or write. Some will sculpt a station for the way of the cross, design a book cover, plant a garden of peace and beauty, or cook a sustaining, delicious meal.

We must strive to be sustained by God's love—for us and for that which we create. When the negative voices interfere, we must say, "This work is of God. Now you go away!"

For Journaling and Reflection

❧ Is it easy or hard for you to accept that you have creative talents? Journal about what your talents are and how you can use them.

❧ Describe the negative voices in your life. When do you hear them, and where do they come from? What do they say? How can you counteract them?

❧ What would you do in your creative and spiritual life if you knew you could not fail? What small steps can you take today to move toward that goal?

16

A Different Way to Look at Life

We should pay close attention to the whole train of our thoughts. If the beginning, middle, and end are all good and tend to what is wholly good, it is a sign of the good angel. But if the train of the thoughts which a spirit causes ends up in something evil or diverting, or in something less good than what the soul was originally proposing to do; or further, if it weakens, disquiets, or disturbs the soul, by robbing it of the peace, tranquility, and quiet which it enjoyed earlier, all this is a clear sign that it comes from the evil spirit, and the enemy of our progress and eternal salvation.

IGNATIUS OF LOYOLA, *The Spiritual Exercises*

*A*gnes put her hands over her face as she spoke of her struggles within and sobbed, "Well, I guess you think I am just a sick puppy!"

"No, no sicker than the rest of us, Agnes. You have had a tremendous amount of sadness to deal with."

Just a few sessions with my spiritual directee (the person coming to me for spiritual direction), Agnes, had revealed an incredible amount of trauma, which had started in her infancy when her natural father almost killed her in a fit of violence. Her stepfather rejected Agnes when he divorced her mother. Her mother had committed suicide. Even more sadness and trauma followed, as her brother disappeared and was never heard from again. At each session, as I listened to Agnes, I was more amazed that this woman was walking around apparently so "normal" and productive, and with her faith in God intact. I praised her for her strengths, and I was sure that God was working in her life in hidden ways. Yet there was no denying that her heart was shattered.

Agnes had thought that her life was firmly on track when she married Carl and they adopted two children. She loved Carl very much, and although they had the usual arguments that married couples have, they shared a mutual passionate love and a set of values on which they built their family.

Then the unthinkable happened. Carl was stricken with cancer. He died over a two-year period, leaving Agnes alone with her children. This had happened nine years ago, and in some ways, Agnes was still grieving. Other relationships had never worked out, and each milestone with her children brought back the freshness of Carl's loss.

We sat in my upstairs bedroom, which I used for spiritual-direction sessions. I hoped that the blue gray carpet and soft yellow walls would be soothing to my friends who visited here. I had layered delicate prints and stripes on the bed, where sat a wise old sock monkey my grandmother had made. A window let in light from the peak of the ceiling. On my desk I had placed an antique embroidered linen cloth and a picture of the pieta. When I expected visitors, I tried to put fresh flowers on my desk and light candles. These are simple things, yet I believe that where there is beauty, God's image is evoked. All I could do was set the stage; the work was up to God. Now Agnes shifted in her chair as she spoke about her feelings toward this God.

"When Mary Jeanne [her daughter] went for her first day of junior high, I said to God, 'Carl should be here, God! Where is her daddy, and why did you take him? I mean, my goodness, she already was given away by her biological family! Now, God takes the daddy who adopted her! What kind of God is that?'"

"Agnes, you are still in the grief process, and you're still angry, and that is just where you are and what you have to take to God. It's okay."

"After nine years?" she demanded. "Don't you think that's a little much?"

For some reason, which neither of us could have anticipated, we both dissolved into laughter, which broke the tension and seemed to direct the conversation in a different direction.

"There is something I never told you. Carl had cancer when I met him."

"What?" I was amazed. I had thought that this cancer was a surprise after their marriage.

"Yes. He almost didn't marry me. He said that if he went into remission, he would. I said I didn't care. I wanted him under any circumstances, but he was adamant."

"And what happened?"

"Well, I bought a dress and planned a wedding. I prayed so hard, and I had faith that Carl would go into remission, and he did."

I sat back in my chair, at a loss for words. Finally, I said, "Agnes, how long did his remission last?"

"For thirteen years. For thirteen happy years."

Then, in my enthusiasm, I probably said too much. "Agnes, don't you see what this means? Those thirteen years were a gift to you and to Carl. It was a time that could easily never have been. Thirteen years of happiness, and two years to say good-bye. Some people don't get that."

"I know. I know. I used to remember that. I forgot, I guess. I just wanted it to go on and on, but it was thirteen happy years. And he was able, after that time, to die in our arms at home. His death was peaceful. Nothing left unsaid. Another gift to us."

"I just wonder if you can recast your thinking a little now," I said. "Maybe you can go to God and talk about the gift of that thirteen years. I don't blame you for wanting it to last and for your wanting to continue to raise you children with Carl. I would have wanted the very same thing, and I would have been devastated when it didn't happen. But, I am really struck by this revelation. It just seems to put things in a different light."

Anger. Gratitude. Confusion. Darkness. Radiance. Despair. All these emotions can, at different times, characterize our relationship with God. Fr. William Barry, who writes a great deal on Ignatian spirituality, encourages us to come clean with God, to tell him everything. After all, and I paraphrase him, God already knows what is in our hearts. We do not protect God by withholding information. We just short-circuit our relationship with him, since honesty is a key component of any relationship. We must mourn our losses. We must allow our feelings to be. And yet, I wonder, when do we get stuck? When do we allow our spirits to weaken too much?

In *The Spiritual Exercises*, Ignatius wrote with infinite care and beautiful subtlety about the inner spirits that come forth as we pray and try to walk the spiritual path. Through careful attention to his words, and through prayer and journaling, we can discern the workings of spirits in our own lives. And we can fully express our disappointments, anger, and grief as well as our gratitude. We can walk in an honest, grateful way, our hand in the hand of Sustaining Love.

For Journaling and Reflection

❧ What has been the most serious loss in your life? How have you worked through your feelings about this loss? What part, if any, has faith played in this process?

❧ What are the great gifts of your life? In what ways do you express gratitude to God?

❧ Reread the opening quote of this chapter. Write about any thoughts you have about the working of the spirits in your life.

❧ How does God sustain your life in everyday ways?

17

The Incarnate Life

I will smell the fragrance and taste the infinite sweetness and
charm of the Divinity, of the soul, of its virtues, and of every-
thing there. . . . I will, so to speak, embrace and kiss the places
where the persons walk or sit.

IGNATIUS OF LOYOLA, *The Spiritual Exercises*

Another cool front rolled into muggy South Louisiana on
a late September day and dispersed the steamy air. As I
walked outside, I struggled with the depression that had engulfed
me since the September 11 tragedies in New York, Washington,
D.C., and Pennsylvania. My thoughts churned inside my head.
If life could be snuffed out so easily, without any warning, what
sense did anything make? Where was God? How would all those
families make it through the loss of their loved ones? My depression had taken the form of a trauma-induced nervousness, a
shaking of my core, of those truths I took for granted. It was
easing some as time passed, but tears came easily. Emotions
floated close to the surface.

However, I had been assured by all of our national leaders that it was our civic duty to go on with our lives, and I wanted to allow my heart to lighten. My depression was not helping anyone. I resolutely went to my car to unload the chrysanthemums and simple clay pots I had recently purchased; fall has always meant chrysanthemums to me. I placed the pots filled with their bright yellow, white, and burgundy flowers along my brick walk. It was a cool and bright day, the power of which is hard to explain unless you have endured endless summer days of ninety degrees and 90 percent humidity. I felt guilty enjoying these simple pleasures when so many people would never have the chance to do so again. And yet, what was the choice? I couldn't live under the bed.

As I later walked into the kitchen, I noticed that Dee had chosen a perfect persimmon a few days earlier that sat in the window becoming too soft. I mashed it up for a persimmon cake. I added applesauce, flour, butter, sugar, and eggs and admired the soft orange batter. I placed the cake in the oven and called Beau, our young bulldog, to lick the bowl. I smiled as his body shook with delight when he lapped up the sweet remains of the batter.

As I started browning a garlicky roast, I felt full of a sorrowful love, a sense of the great sweetness of life, the gifts of life: the persimmon, sitting cool and heavy in my hand; magenta mums and cake batter; the shiny russet and white of Beau, who sat in the warm sunlight that streamed through the windows. I heard the squabble of the squirrels on the roof, like children at recess, and the whoosh of the cars in the distance; I enjoyed the fragrance of the spicy roast and the unmistakable aroma of a cake in the oven. Life was good. Life was so good.

My heart mourned again for those three thousand innocent people who would not sense the wonders of the earth again. But, at that very moment I prayed that they were held safe in the arms of God. That all the lost were in a better place. So many of those people had expressed love in quick phone calls home just before the end. And as in love they had died, in love they were received by the God who also sustains us on this Earth. Love is eternal even as everything else passes away.

The quote that began this chapter, written by Ignatius in *The Spiritual Exercises,* applies to both the heavenly plan of the Incarnation and the traveling of Mary and Joseph to Bethlehem to receive the birth of Jesus. For Jesus, life began in that little stable, surrounded by the warmth of the living animals and the scent of hay, the gentle touch of his mother. He came into a life of the world, a life of the senses. He came fully into a life of joy and pain. He walked the dusty roads and thoroughly enjoyed a good meal. He drank sweet wine at weddings and laughed and grieved with his friends. He lived a life overflowing with love, a life that would be brutally ended by those who could not understand him. Yet through it all, God sustained him. Ignatius said in wonder, "Jesus did it all for me!"

Ignatius tells us to taste with love that heavenly plan, that holy family, to taste Jesus' life. For in that life exists all our lives, the essence and vitality of both body and spirit. Ours is an incarnate faith, and the blessings and the sorrows of both body and soul fill our lives.

For Journaling and Reflection

❀ What events in your life or the world have caused trauma and grief? What has God meant to you during these times?

❀ Why do you think that Jesus came to earth and took human form? Do you think he enjoyed his life? Explain.

❀ What in this life sustains you and gives you joy?

❀ How do your five senses contribute to your happiness?

18

My Journey Has Not Been Easy

I can well believe . . . because of the many enemies and diffi-culties you meet with in God's service . . . you are feeling over-whelmed. For the love of God our Lord, try to keep going forward. . . . [a]nd so for the love of God let us make every effort in him, since we owe him so much. For we tire of receiv-ing his gifts, much sooner than he tires of giving. [May our] own weak and sorry spirits be made joyful in his praise.

IGNATIUS OF LOYOLA, IN A LETTER TO AGNES PASCUAL

*I*n a recent letter to me, my friend and fellow musician from Pennsylvania, Ann, wrote: "How does one begin to tell the story of a heartbreak? The pain and hurt, though healed some-what by time, are once again brought to the surface as these words are written.

"In March 1998, after twenty-seven years of marriage, a life-giving, Christ-centered partnership, my husband suddenly announced that he didn't love me, had never really been happy in our life together. He offered me no opportunity for counsel-ing or attempts at reconciliation. He had made his decision, and I alone had to deal with it.

"I was stripped of every belief I owned: faith, security in unconditional love, the sanctity of my marriage vows, self-respect, and dignity. The feelings of rejection were overwhelming. I fell into a deep, deep depression and over time, as the pain did not lessen, I planned my death. I fell fully into a dark night of despair. I wrote letters of explanation to those I loved as I prepared to carry out my plan in a few days.

"But, I only thought I was alone. That Sunday evening as I tried to sleep, God began his plan of salvation for me. This date was March 15, the anniversary of the suicide of one of my former students. I think I may have heard this student, Mike, speak to me. Or perhaps it was God or one of his angels. I also saw the face of my dear friend, Kathy, who had made me promise not to hurt myself, but to call her instead. No matter, I distinctly heard a voice tell me to get out of bed, get dressed, and go to the hospital for help! Now! I did, and my long, long journey of healing began."

Ann was ill in both spirit and body. A disorder of the pancreas caused her to lose weight and become very ill. I had met Ann the year before her crisis, at a guitar school and while she was still happily married. When I saw her the next year at the same guitar school, I was shocked. This pretty, vivacious lady had clearly undergone trauma. Her skin tone was yellow, her thinness was skeletal, and her face was clouded and drawn with inner pain. But Bobby Fisher, the guitarist who heads the school, had told her, "Come, Ann. You need to be here. I know it is a part of your healing."

I watched in wonder through the week as Ann humbly accepted the love of those around her. Her tears flowed and flowed. People held her and prayed with her and over her. By the end of the week she was radiant. I was awed by her transformation.

I saw the workings of Christ, the workings of the unconditional love she thought she had lost forever.

In her letter, Ann outlined in gratitude what sustained and healed her during her crisis: "The overflowing abundance of prayers from friends, family, and even strangers. I was on prayer chains across the country. People I didn't even know were praying for me.

"Next, I praise God for dear friends and family who supported me financially when I was left with nothing. God's amazing grace sustained me through them. My inner desire to return to music, to sing and play my guitar again for the Lord, gave me something to live for. I give thanks for the belief in me that others expressed. They told me that I was going to make it. They said I had what I needed to survive. I did. It was my trust in God.

"My wonderful doctors aided me in my physical and emotional healing. My priest friends helped me to heal spiritually.

"Finally, I bless two male friends who taught me I could love again and be loved. That I am good and beautiful because God created a miracle when he made me!

"There is hope," says Ann. "Just turn your life over to the Master Designer. I believe that God wants me to be happy. I see his presence in every bend of the road. I really didn't experience more than I could bear. My healed life is proof of this."

Ann is seeking an annulment today; after almost four years, a new love, James, has come into her life, and she hopes someday to remarry. James's wife was diagnosed with cancer as Ann's marriage was ending. James was in a deep and long-lasting anguish. Ann has known James for years, and they sang and played in church choirs together. Their renewed friendship was platonic for a long time. Then, as Ann said, "I had come into

James's life to comfort him as I had been comforted, to share Christ's love. James now teases that I 'stayed on' as a new romance. Only God could have designed this. Both James and I have had to endure the pain of our paths to be who we are today. We are walking carefully, keeping God and Christ at our center. We believe that God is designing a special way for us to serve him. We just await his timing and his word."

I folded Ann's letter with deep satisfaction. In her story is revealed the God who heals, saves, and sustains. Ignatius comforted his longtime friend Agnes Pascual as she grieved the loss of a deceased friend. Agnes had reached out to St. Ignatius, doubtless because of his spiritual muscle. He counseled her about the God who still gives gifts, even when we tire of receiving them.

As I pondered Ann's story, one thing stood out clearly. Many people offered their help to her, and she humbly received it. I believe that this made the difference in her experience; this turned her path from despair to healing and sustenance. God, no doubt, sends us help through others. Sometimes it is difficult for us to receive that help. No one wants pity, and offers of help can be perceived in this way. I come from a line of rather proud and independent people, so it is often hard for me to accept help from others. Sometimes I struggle alone when I don't need to.

Ignatius would have been pleased with Ann, I believe, that she graciously received God's gifts—those gifts he never tires of giving. And since I know her well, I am assured that, in turn, she will shower others with Christ's generosity.

For Journaling and Reflection

❀ How do other people sustain you in daily life? Write about those who bring you spiritual gifts.

❀ Is it difficult or easy for you to accept help from others? Why?

❀ Describe how other people helped or hindered your healing process after a conflict in your family or other relationships.

❀ Journal about any change you are facing, whether it is a gradual or sudden change.

19

Personal Resurrection

The first Holy Saturday, [Mary] alone, never doubted that her son's promise of raising himself from the grave would be realized.

JOHN A. HARDON, S.J., *Retreat with the Lord*

Mary had to live by [the] faith [that], "he sets free the souls of the just . . . he appears in body and soul."

IGNATIUS OF LOYOLA, QUOTED IN *Retreat with the Lord*

Mary Magdalene had been a notorious sinner. Loving the Truth, she cleansed her sins with her tears. Unlike the disciples who fled, she did not flee. In the great strength of her love, she came to the tomb of the Lord.

ST. GREGORY, QUOTED IN *Retreat with the Lord*

I was amazed that we had driven to the heart of such a scene. The sun was low in the sky, casting deep blue shadows over the gray blue lake. Ducks were swooping into their nesting areas, their feathered bodies gliding on the water, creating long, slick crescents of wave and shadow. Further to the west, the sky was shot through with the lavender and pink of sunset.

"Wow," I said to Dee as we stopped our rented camper. "I can't believe that we can park right here!"

I searched in the camper for something to feed the ducks and finally went out somewhat ashamed with potato chips. "They probably don't need this salt," I said.

As I balanced on the water's edge, I said hello to the young blonde woman who had emerged from her camper, bread for the ducks in hand. A cap sat jauntily on her head. She wore an oversized navy sweatshirt and well-worn jeans.

She smiled at me. "In a minute I'll start a fire in this ring," she said. "This is my favorite time of the day."

We introduced ourselves—her name was Allison—and chitchatted about where I was from and how I came to be at the park. Allison sat with me by the fire and suddenly began to speak from her heart.

"After my divorce and my hysterectomy, I began to come out here often," she said. Divorce and hysterectomy in one short sentence! What pain this woman had been through.

Allison continued. "My sister and brother-in-law keep this camper in the park, and I began to use it. It's so beautiful here, and I have been forced to seek the simple things in life. When I was recovering from my surgery, I was so low. I asked God for a sign. I said, 'Where are you, God? Do you even exist, this God I have prayed to for my whole life?'"

Allison paused, and I waited. The earth was settling down in earnest now. The cries of the wood ducks and mallards were quieting, and the night call of the dove echoed and faded. As the night grew chilly, we welcomed the fire's warmth.

"Well, one day I went to the grocery store. It was one of my first outings after the surgery. When I was getting my groceries out of the car, a butterfly landed on my shoulder. Would you believe that this butterfly went inside with me while I put up my groceries? And, would you believe that I came back out and it still perched on me, with just a tiny flutter of its wings? I put out my hand, and it climbed aboard." Allison moved closer to the fire and pulled the sweatshirt down over her knees.

"That butterfly must have stayed with me for thirty minutes. Maybe to some people, that wouldn't be much. But to me, it was my sign. You see, dreams of what my life was going to be had died. That day I dared to believe that God was with me and that God was teaching me to start enjoying the little things, like a beautiful butterfly. Well, maybe they're not such little things.

"So, I started staying out here, and my body got stronger, and I met a lot of simple, good-hearted people. And I watch the ducks; I know each of them now. I know which ones come and go, and stay, which are the leaders. I know that the black geese that hide under the branches are shy, so I try to get a little food to them. And I look for butterflies. My mom and sisters really don't understand." She smiled. "But this is my path, now."

The next morning, Allison had gone to work. I went outside and placed my watercolors on the picnic table. I tried several times to create a butterfly. The final try was somewhat of a success, I think. In the faint outline of its wings I placed the warm colors of the sunset, the blue of the water. The colors spilled outside the lines and filled the space around them. I left this butterfly for Allison, and I hope she believes the Spirit gave it to her, for I believe the Spirit did.

For centuries the butterfly has been a symbol of Christ's resurrection. The caterpillar appears lifeless in the chrysalis, yet it emerges days later, transformed with great beauty and purpose.

Ignatius emphasized that when Christ emerged from his tomb, he appeared to the women first. He came to announce, as the Spirit did to Allison, that although life had changed and some dreams had died, greater dreams were present in the Resurrection. And the women listened and believed, just as Allison did. Perhaps they believed easily because they had so little else to cling to. Theirs was a world not of power or prestige but of hope.

And so it is with Allison, and so with us: as we release lost dreams—the forms into which we have tried to force our lives—we can embrace the beauty of the life that is. This is the power of the resurrected Christ, hidden in nature, visible in the kindness of others. It is a life mysteriously sustained by him in our hearts.

For Journaling and Reflection

❦ How have your goals and dreams changed over the years?

❦ What symbols are important to you? You may want to write about personal symbols (such as the butterfly) or Christian symbols such as water, light, the cross, or Lenten ashes.

❦ In what small ways does God send you consolation for lost dreams?

❦ How have new activities, plans, and dreams filled your life? Do you need to find new ones? What could you do to help yourself in this quest?

20

The God Who Sustains Us

The enemy's general practice with persons who desire and are beginning to serve God our Lord is to throw up obstacles and impediments. . . . He says for example, "How are you going to live a lifetime of such penance . . . a lonely life, with no respite?"
IGNATIUS OF LOYOLA, IN A LETTER TO TERESA REJADELL

Taken out of context, [Christ's words make] God is seen as being most pleased with us when we are giving ourselves a hard time and our holiness is measured by our ability to endure suffering. This is a total distortion of Jesus' message.
GERARD W. HUGHES, *Seven Weeks for the Soul*

*A*soft autumn rain is falling, and unusual things are bursting into bloom. The sweet olive beside the walk is filled with scent as fall rushes by to meet winter. Beside my office door the hardy sage that I planted years ago keeps reseeding and is now blooming pink.

I find such comfort in nature, as it placidly lives out its destiny, never questioning or complaining. We are not like nature, nor are we meant to be. It is our destiny to question and ask why, to hurt. And the answers are not easy ones. Our concepts of fairness must fall, crumbled to the muddy ground. We are left with questions and with the task of listening to God's voice in our lives.

God comes in different ways to different people, and not always in the ways we plan or ask for. The surrendering of our will to God's will can be painful and exhausting, and yet it is the only way to the freedom we seek. In that surrender are the peace and joy that we long for. This is a daily task! To paraphrase Gerard Hughes, we should give time to that which brings us to life and helps us to cherish God's creation.

Throughout Ignatian spirituality, the belief is expressed that God constantly creates and sustains the world. Every tree grows, every bird lays its eggs, because God's hand actively sustains life. It is the same with humans: we breathe each breath because God wills it.

Ignatius was severely tempted by inner voices when he began his serious Christian journey. The voices said, "How can you live like this for seventy more years?" The voices can be compared to Peter's, when he said to Christ, "Oh, not you, Lord. Surely you won't have to die." In both cases, the holy ones said, "Get thee behind me, Satan." For they knew that we cannot long contemplate the future when we are in pain. When we are in difficulty and sorrow, it is time to ask for God's sustenance—on a day-by-day, even moment-by-moment basis.

And in our joys and our service, in the resurrections that follow our deaths and loss, God is there to sustain us. God wishes joy for us, and he is surely sending it in each breath.

For Journaling and Reflection

❧ When you pray to God for healing, what do you say? Try writing your own prayer.

❧ Do you believe that God sustains creation daily? In what ways?

❧ How do you depend on God for the day-to-day ability to maintain your life?

PRAYER TO THE GOD
WHO SUSTAINS

God, I know you are breathing life into me,
moment by moment.
May I not be so attached to my possessions,
my plans, even my loved ones,
that I fail to see your love,
upholding all that lives.

Sustain me, my God.
Send me hope when I feel far from you.
And when I am rejoicing,
let it be your name that is ever on my lips.

21

Casey's Conversion

Up to the age of twenty-six he was a man given to the vanities of the world.

IGNATIUS OF LOYOLA, *The Autobiography*

*S*haron O'Neill and I sat with our earphones on, doing another show for Radio Maria. Our guest was Casey Johnston, a fellow choir member and an old friend. Casey was the deacon in our community, and he was appearing on the show to talk about his conversion experience.

Casey is a slightly plump, engaging man of fifty, with a ready laugh and brown eyes that actually twinkle. We call ourselves spiritual brother and sister, and our birthdays are both in June. "We're both Geminis and a lot alike," says Casey with a smile. "But, of course, we good Catholics don't believe in that stuff. Ha!"

I had told Casey to share as much of his early life as he wished. "My dad had such a hard time," he began. "He was basically an orphan who joined the military when he was seventeen. He was captured in the Philippines and was beaten and starved for several years. He lost his hearing because a land mine blew up at his feet. And he was scarred within, badly.

"He met and married my mom after the war. My mom worked for the Jesuits in Grand Coteau, and there were always priests at our house for lunch." Casey looked down, shaking his head and chuckling, "My dad gave them a hard time. But you know Jesuits, they love to debate, so it wasn't a problem. But neither Dad nor the priests would ever back down.

"After I was born my dad lost his sight, due to the malnutrition he had suffered in the war." Sharon and I shook our heads. If Casey's father had argued that a God of love did not exist, we could see why.

Casey continued, "There was not a lot of emotional connection with my dad, and it affected me, yet I was a good little Catholic boy until the age of seventeen or so. I have to say that ages seventeen to thirty-two are a black hole in my life—kind of a blank. Except that I married my beautiful wife during that time. That was worth so much.

"I played in a rock band, and we traveled all over the Southeast, trying to make it. We all lived together in an old house in Duson, an old farmhouse, and the front porch was our trash can. A lot of bottles lay piled on that porch. Yep, we didn't live too clean a life then.

"Cindy, now my wife, came one night to hear me play. She was with her sister. Word got around that she liked this ol' keyboard player, so this ol' keyboard player asked her to dance. I still remember the song we danced to. It was 'Beware the Queen of Spades.'

"Cindy was a devout Catholic. We lived in Milton, a stone's throw from the church, and she went every Sunday. I slept in, or I took a walk, right by the church. After about three years I noticed that Cindy wasn't going to church all that much any-more. She'd go maybe twice a month, if that.

"I was walking one Sunday morning, and as I passed the church a voice came to me as clear as day: 'Casey Johnston, if you want to send your own sorry self to hell, you can. But now you are dragging your beautiful, sweet wife down with you!' I was so convicted at that moment. I knew, I knew I had to change, to repent.

"Believe it or not, just as I stopped after hearing this voice, the priest came out of the church. I ran up to him. 'Father! I have to make my confession! Now!' The priest said, 'Casey, I have a funeral in a few minutes. Come back tomorrow and I will give you all the time you need.' I met the next day with Fr. Primeaux. He could not have been more loving, more compassionate, more welcoming. He sat with me for three hours. I have never felt so wonderful as when he performed absolution. I was home again."

We discussed the couple's struggle to conceive a child and their success using natural family planning and prayers to the Blessed Mother. "C. J., our son, was conceived on Mardi Gras," said Casey, a mischievous twinkle in his eye, "after six years of trying."

Casey told us about his long struggle to finish deacon studies. I, myself, had been with Casey in church when he had pointed out a family and said, "See that little family? I blessed their marriage and baptized all three children last year. What an incredible privilege!"

Adjusting his earphones, Casey paused in his story. His eyes met mine. "Our God is a God of welcoming, forgiving love," he said in a choked voice. "I never dreamed I could be used by him in this way. I threw away a lot of years."

"Maybe not, Casey," I said. "Maybe that was just your path."

When Ignatius experienced his conversion, he wanted to tell everyone that mortal sin was death. How surprised his brother and others who had known him were when they encountered this new Ignatius. As are many of the newly converted, he may have been a little hard to take. Ignatius relentlessly cast aside that which caused him to stumble, that which stood in the way of his full commitment to his God. Yet he was never far from memories of his early life, his perceptions of his sinfulness. And as he traveled the higher path, he wanted to take everyone he met with him.

At Manresa Ignatius spent a year as a penitent and lived through storms of desolation that led to a more lasting consolation of soul. He experienced the God of welcoming and forgiving love, and perhaps this caused a softening in him. When he later worked in Rome, he saw the prostitutes not as sinners to be shunned but as souls of Christ to be saved. He never turned away from needy people in lowly places. He reached out in love, just as Christ did. For Ignatius knew that in Christ, "all is well."

For Journaling and Reflection

❧ What wrongdoings of yours make you particularly uncomfortable? What kind of help have you sought for these matters?

❧ What is your definition of sin? How does it compare to the church's definition of sin?

❊ Describe how you believe sin actually affects people.

❊ Have you experienced a conversion—something that brought you closer to God—an experience small or large? If so, describe it now.

❊ What part of Casey's experience touched you the most? Why?

❊ If you are Catholic, do you take advantage of the sacrament of Reconciliation? Why or why not?

22

Amber's Dad Faces His Death

One should ask God our Lord for what one desires, namely, grace to recall how often one has fallen into the particular sin or fault, in order to correct it in the future. Then one should make the first examination, exacting an account of oneself with regard to the particular matter.

IGNATIUS OF LOYOLA, *The Spiritual Exercises*

*M*y friend Amber knocked at the door and I called, "Come in!" She stood beside me as I stirred creamy corn-and-broccoli soup and seasoned our romaine lettuce salads. Outside, thunder cracked and the trees swayed in the wind.

"Are you ready for your interview, Amber?" I teased, as we sat at the table sipping tea.

"Fire away." She smiled.

Amber settled into the story of her childhood. "My dad could sell anything. My daughter, Stacey, is just like him! I didn't get that gene."

Amber continued her narration, telling me that things were very rocky at her house much of the time. "Dad did not treat

Mom the way that he should have, if you know what I mean. Mom knew about his bad deeds, and they fought loudly about it. I became the family peacekeeper that I still am today. I was little mother to my younger brothers, too.

"And yet, I remember a time in Opelousas that my childhood was idyllic. We lived beside a big park, and the dads would hang rope swings and build us bridges over the ditches to play on. There was a gang of us. It was like something you would see on television. Yep," she continued, sipping her soup, "that's life. Up and down. Good and bad.

"My parents separated after I was grown and married. Then my dad had a lot of heart trouble. He had heart attacks and surgery.

"I never felt a lot of emotional connection with Daddy. But he always helped me. He would come to my house and fix things. I guess that was his way of showing affection. I was pretty angry with him for his history of bad behavior, yet he tried. He was a pretty good grandfather.

"My parents got back together after a long separation. I didn't really know why. But then began a period that I would call 'Held in God's Hands.' It was strange, the way it all happened.

"One Sunday, my dad called all of his family over to the house. He had done most of the cooking for a big Sunday dinner; Mom just helped. All of us children and grandchildren were there. We talked and played games. We laughed and connected.

"After dinner, my dad gathered us and began to talk. It was not like him at all. He told us that he had gone to the church. He told us that he had seen Fr. Louie."

"What was your father's faith life like?" I asked.

"Poof! As far as I knew, it didn't exist. Oh, he went to church with us sometimes when we were growing up. But you know, he didn't have a lot of accountability about his life that I knew about, and so he had no credibility as far as I was concerned.

"After that dinner we all sat, entranced, as Dad told us that Fr. Louie had spoken to him for a long time. Fr. Louie had heard his confession and had counseled him and given him absolution. As he spoke, we wondered, *Who is this man?*

Amber twisted a piece of bread in her fingers. "He told us that he was at peace. That he loved us and was at peace. We told him that we loved him, too. Our hearts were touched by his sincerity. We told him that we were glad that he was finding this peace and forgiveness.

"One week later my brothers came to my door. One brother told me that my father had died suddenly at home while my brother tried to administer CPR. I had the flu and I had a little baby. I was in a daze. I could not cope, and I could not believe what I was hearing. I was not at all expecting him to die.

"Now, a lot of time has passed. I wonder how Dad knew, or if Dad knew that his time on earth was ending. I don't believe he was just avoiding God's wrath. I think he was truly sorry for his mistakes. I believe that he also wanted peace for himself and us. I have had such tremendous peace knowing that he was all right with God and us at the end. I guess that was his gift, this gift of peace. We really didn't have unfinished business. It was a miracle for all of us."

Ignatius was anointed for death several times in his life. Toward the end of his life he forbade himself to think about death, as the idea of it gave him such consolation. Isn't this the model for all of us Christians—that we face death fearlessly?

As we grow in faith and become more mature on our journey, we can turn our eyes to the final end. For surely, we all must die. The only question is, what will our death be like? Will we go peacefully, having given peace to those around us? Can we look forward to seeing God face to face? Or will we still be clinging to this life and to our cares, vices, and pettiness? Well, even if we are, we can know that God is ever willing to forgive us, to welcome us home again.

For Journaling and Reflection

✤ If today were your last day on earth, what would you do? Can you do some of these things now?

✤ How do you feel about Amber's family's willingness to forgive? Would you have been so forgiving?

✤ When you think of your own death, what are your fears? Your consolations?

✤ Do you have a visual image of heaven? Write about it in detail.

23

Making Sense of Anger

For just as the good spirit is chiefly the one who guides and counsels us in time of consolation, so it is the evil spirit who does this in time of desolation. By following his counsels we can never find a way to a right decision.

IGNATIUS OF LOYOLA, *The Spiritual Exercises*

Connie's hand gripped the phone receiver with white knuckles. "No, Charlie, I don't think I wrote the contract that way. I never write them that way, but I am at home and I don't have it in front of me." Connie was somewhat new to the real-estate business, but she was already highly successful.

The irate older man on the other end of the line shot back, "Yes, you did. I don't have it either, but I remember. You'd better get your act together! I've been doing this for a long time, and I can tell you, you'd better be more careful and take care of business!"

Connie put the phone back in its cradle, her head aching. Charlie was the most difficult agent she had ever worked with. He seemed to thrive on power rather than on serving the needs of his customers. He put Connie down at every turn. Connie breathed slowly and reached for a little book of prayers that she had nearby. She read one aloud. Then she tried to forget the incident.

A couple of days passed, during which Charlie acknowledged in an offhanded way that the contract had not been written as he had claimed. But he certainly did not apologize. Then Connie needed an appraisal report on the property that her clients were purchasing. She called Charlie over a period of four days. Her calls were never returned, and her clients were becoming frantic. Finally, she reached Charlie. "Have you been ill?" she asked sincerely.

"No," the man shot back. "Why?"

"Well, I have been calling you for four days trying to get that appraisal report, and you have not returned my calls. My clients don't know what to think."

"You come down to the office right now, Connie," said Charlie. "We have a few things to get straight."

When Connie walked into Charlie's office, he began to scold her harshly, saying that Connie didn't know a thing about what she was doing, that she was pushy and unprofessional, that Charlie had fifteen more days in which to legally supply the report. Connie stood in the office, stunned. Then she turned and retreated into the hall.

"Come back in here, Connie! I am not through with you!"

Connie stepped back into the older man's office, and the berating continued. Finally, Connie opened her mouth. "I am not taking any more of this, you b------!" As soon as the words left her mouth, Connie was mortified. She was a Christian! She was a good person—well, maybe not. She went to her car in tears.

Connie is a dear friend of mine, and she told me this story recently as we sat in another friend's home, watching the festival and street fair that was going on in the courtyard just beyond us. Connie was sitting, now relaxed, on the sofa, and she shook her head.

"I apologized to Charlie several times, but I couldn't shake the feeling that I was a bad person. I began to beat myself up. I beat myself up all week. I wanted to just quit, or hide, or do something to escape my own feelings of disgust."

"Gosh, Connie," I said, "I'm getting mad just hearing the story. I can't imagine what it was like being on the receiving end of all that abuse. It seems to me you withstood it for quite a while."

"Well, I let myself down, I felt. I lowered my own standards; that's what I couldn't forgive myself for. But that changed today at Mass."

"What happened at Mass?"

"Well, I was going to communion, and I was filled with self-disgust. I thought about not even going. Then I felt God. God was like a warm wind, a wonderful energy that flowed into me, into my chest around my heart. I felt God say, *Connie. I forgave you long ago. Forgive yourself.*

"I forgave myself! My heart completely lightened. I received communion with so much gratitude." Connie's face was shining as she related this story. "I call that a big 'Ping,'" she said. "God pings us, and it is like a sweet arrow to the heart. We just have to finally listen to him."

I can attest from my own experience and from working with others that anger is one of the biggest challenges, emotionally, that many of us Christians face. We know intellectually that feeling anger is not a sin. And yet, we have no idea what to do with anger. When do we speak up? How much do we forbear? There are no easy rules to follow. And, like Connie, many of us stuff and stuff our anger until it explodes in ways we regret.

In retrospect, could Connie have been more assertive in the beginning with Charlie? She could have said, "Charlie, please don't speak to me that way; I don't speak to others disrespect-fully, and I don't allow others to speak to me disrespectfully." Would this have helped? Perhaps it would have dissipated some of Connie's anger before it exploded, causing her shame.

Should Connie have called in a supervisor early on to medi-ate? Would she have looked like the company tattletale? Every day, in workplaces everywhere, people face such choices. And in the heart of our working lives is the spiritual journey where we often feel anger that we don't know how to process. We read in our Scriptures about the dangers of acting in anger, and yet sup-pressing all that anger (as we try to be "perfect" Christians) can really depress us and sap our energy. All we can do is keep try-ing. Through prayer we can refute the evil spirits who tell us that we are bad when we express our anger. The emotion of anger serves a useful purpose, often telling us when things are not right or when we are being taken advantage of. And we can try to express that anger in appropriate, productive ways. We can learn what it is to be assertive rather than aggressive.

The great psychologist Carl Jung studied the work of Ignatius. He thought that Ignatius's work on the discernment of spirits was insightful and helpful in his own work. It takes time and quiet to discern these spirits within us.

It is important that we not believe what the negative voices within us say, and we must not make major decisions when we are feeling desolate. Decisions made or actions taken in desola-tion can distance us from God. We need to pray, plan, and dis-cern the actions to take. As Connie said, "We must listen to God."

For Journaling and Reflection

❀ How do you handle your anger? Has this worked for you? If not, in what ways can you change how you handle anger?

❀ How do you think God feels about our anger?

❀ Describe a time when you were on the receiving end of someone else's anger.

❀ Describe an angry incident that you regret. Consider how you might seek healing and forgiveness for any wounds and sins you carry that are related to anger.

24

Everyday Blessings

First Point: To his beloved disciples he speaks apart about the eight beatitudes: "Blessed are the poor in spirit, the meek, the merciful . . . the peacemakers."

IGNATIUS OF LOYOLA, *The Spiritual Exercises*

$\mathcal{M}$y husband, Dee, and I were leaving the barbecue restaurant. I had a paper bag of sandwiches in one hand and a Styrofoam container of rice dressing in the other. My husband was paying the bill. The owner, a friendly man of about sixty or so asked, "Do you want a bag for that rice dressing?"

"Yes, I guess I will take a bag," I replied.

"You have a bag," said my husband.

"He meant for the dressing," I said.

"It's right there in your hand," Dee said, shortly.

I stopped and looked ruefully at the restaurant owner. "My husband and I are not communicating very well." I sighed.

His wife, standing beside him in a sauce-stained apron, laughed. "Well, you can just join the rest of us in that, honey!"

"Yep," said her husband, nodding at two other waitresses who looked up and smiled, "This seems to be the day." He chuckled as he handed me a bag.

I felt suddenly embraced by the human family. It would not be an exaggeration to say that these comments turned my day around as I experienced the truth of the phrase "Blessed are the meek, the poor in spirit." Blessed are those who share their struggles and their imperfections and thereby help others.

How wonderful it is when we can let down our masks and admit our humanness, when we can confess that relationships can be a struggle. Healing can come to us as we release our rigid expectations, share our frustrations, and freely participate in the flow of life. Our God is a God of welcoming love. He accepts us as we are and then calls us to more—more love, more life.

Ignatius had a life that was built on sharing his faith with others. After his deep spiritual experiences, he did not retreat to the mountaintop to savor God alone and in silence. He immediately sought to bring the truths he had discovered to many people in his life. His loving desire to share often got him into trouble because he was not an ordained priest when he began and many people were suspicious of him. But that didn't stop his love. He willingly suffered deprivation, illness, and scorn to bring his understanding of the gospel to others.

My story of our little exchange in the barbecue restaurant is humble and down-to-earth, but then so was Ignatius in many ways. It is evidenced in his letters that no detail in the lives of his friends and coworkers was brushed off as unimportant. In his letters he lovingly answered all their questions and comforted them in their woes. Despite his extraordinary talent and drive, he was truly one meek and poor of spirit, a peacemaker who saw God. He welcomed others as God welcomes us.

For Journaling and Reflection

❧ Is it easy for you to share your failures and frustrations with others? Why or why not?

❧ Write about any perfectionism—or nonchalance—that has caused friction in a relationship. Describe how you dealt with it.

❧ What do the words "Blessed are the meek" mean to you? Before you journal about this, you might read the Sermon on the Mount in your Bible: Matthew 5–7.

25

St. Peter among Us

Simon Peter, who had a sword, drew it and struck the high priest's servant, cutting off his right ear.

JOHN 18:10

All four evangelists give the account of Peter's denial of Jesus. Each time someone asked him if he was not one of his disciples. A combination of respect, fear, and cowardice got the upper hand. Not only did he deny that he even knew Jesus, but "he began to curse and swear, 'I do not know the man you speak of' (Mark 14:71)."

JOHN A. HARDON, S.J., *Retreat with the Lord*

*T*he ten women in my living room, all members of our "Water from Stones" class, were struggling. "I don't think I get it," said Martha. "Maybe I'm not spiritual enough."

"No, I'm the least spiritual of the group," said another member, a young second-grade teacher. "In fact, I am sure you are all looking at me thinking, *What is she doing in this class?*"

"You guys are funny," I responded. "Oh, the rest of us would be really spiritually advanced if we were looking down our noses at you! Maybe we need to reflect again about what tuning into the spiritual nature really means. I don't know everything about it either!"

It was at this point that Kathleen, one of the more boisterous members, spoke up. "Listen. I have you all beat! I smoke like a chimney. I can curse like a sailor. I don't drink anymore, but I have a terrible temper. Don't back me in a corner; I'll come at you! Yes, even you nice ladies." She shook her head with a self-deprecating smile. "I'm really not proud of it. I'm not boasting, you understand. This is the personality I deal with every day. It just wears me out."

The room dissolved in laughter. I felt a sudden affection for Kathleen and her delightful honesty. I felt refreshed—and this conversation reminded me of something, but what?

A few days later, as I was running an errand, the answer came to me: Peter! Kathleen reminded me of Peter: strong, someone you would want on your side, feisty, hot-tempered, changeable, honest, and impulsive. These qualities were the rock upon which Jesus built his church.

If we ever doubt that God is a God of welcoming, forgiving love, we can look at the relationship between Jesus and Peter. Peter gave the Lord a lot of trouble. He refused to believe that Jesus could face the cross, causing Christ to call him Satan. He bumbled along, never quite understanding Jesus' mission, yet loving and trusting the man himself. He impulsively cut off a guard's ear when Jesus was arrested, flying in the face of the Lord's obvious policy of nonviolence. But, by far, the most grievous thing that Peter did was to deny Jesus three times. At the time of his master's greatest need, Peter surrendered to his fear. Peter is like us, and we are like him.

Yet Jesus lovingly welcomed Peter back three times with the message "Do you love me? Feed my sheep." His embrace of Peter, despite Peter's many failings, should be a lesson to us all, a lesson in forgiveness and self-acceptance.

Ignatius of Loyola was a complex person. He could be taciturn and unknowable. He was certainly stubborn. He once became angry at his beloved sister-in-law, Magdalena, because she told a minor fib. He would not speak to her for three days! In the time following his initial conversion, he struggled with hatred for himself and harshness toward others. Yet at the River Cardoner, "God taught him as a schoolmaster teaches a child." God was bringing him along, as he does us when we face our complexities and our shadows. In Ignatius's very faults were the seeds of his great gifts. A reading of St. Ignatius's life shows that while his ambition never wavered, he mellowed in other ways. He worried about the health of young Jesuits and wrote at length to comfort others in their sorrows. He began to more fully embrace a God of mercy.

For Journaling and Reflection

❦ Do you accept yourself as you are, or is that difficult for you? Explain.

❦ Do you believe that God shows you unconditional love? If not, why? If so, how does God do this?

❦ What are your faults? Try to think of biblical stories that feature people who also possessed these flaws. Write about those people and about yourself.

26

Developing Spiritual Muscles

I close, praying God our Lord by his infinite clemency to guide you and govern you in all things through his infinite and supreme goodness.
IGNATIUS OF LOYOLA, IN A LETTER TO TERESA REJADELL

Finally, I call consolation every increase of faith, hope, and love and all interior joy that invites and attracts to what is heavenly.
IGNATIUS OF LOYOLA, *The Spiritual Exercises*

*S*oon after our trip to Texas, during which I'd met Allison beside the lake, I entered a time of darkness, triggered by the hurtful actions of a "friend." Other people's reactions to my outbursts about the friend's betrayal increased my distress, and soon the darkness was thickening around my heart.

In the back of my mind, I was also aware that I was thinking about my problem so much that I was prolonging my own misery. I could see the pattern, as much as I didn't want to. Things that would cause others an hour or two of distress and irritation, in my husband's words, knocked me off my horse. And when this happened, I was injured for many days. Even worse, I knew that certain aspects of my personality had helped attract this type of hurtful event.

I can certainly see the irony of this as I try to open others to the love of Christ and to walk with them through their difficulties. Because of my writing and spiritual direction, there was a glimmer of hope that this latest experience had happened for a reason—perhaps that reason was this book. I realized then that I had the opportunity to see if prayer could free my heart, slowly, perhaps, but surely.

On my Texas trip I had purchased a little icon of the Virgin of Guadalupe. When I saw it in a tiny shop, I knew that I had to have it. It had been made in Mexico, and I thought about the loving hands that had painted the bright metal facing around the Virgin's figure.

One day after my problems with my friend began, I was on my sunporch cleaning my glass table. On the table I placed the icon, along with a framed picture of the pietà. A recent watercolor of mine, showing a ship tossed in a storm, also made its way to the table. A new friend had given me a luminary candle, cheerful and yellow, that she had made; it spoke to me of rejoicing. A candle with St. Michael the archangel sat beside it. I needed his strength. A crystal butterfly reminded me of the Resurrection and of Allison's experience.

A recent turn in my prayer life had surprised me. I had begun to pray the rosary after I read a book about it published by Loyola Press. I had originally bought the book out of curiosity about the style and format of Loyola's books. But it seemed that God had other plans than just my gathering of information. After I read the book, there was a movement of recognition in my heart; I purchased a little rosary.

Now I sat, deep in desolation, and began to pray. I used Joyce Rupp's book about Mary, entitled *My Sorrow Is Your Sorrow.* At intervals during the rosary I would read some of the beautiful thoughts and prayers Joyce had written to and about Mary. There was such a large part of me that I longed to heal, not just from this incident, but from the extremes of emotion that sometimes characterize my life. I felt that something important was happening. I was slowly uniting my pain with that of the Holy Family. Not that mine compares, but as one of my personal heroes, Paula D'Arcy, states, "Our pain is our pain. We can't compare it to another's. We can only live through it and heal it."

As I stared at the flickering candles and listened to the drone of my own voice, I felt comforted by the Mother. I visualized her arms around me, just as my own mother would place her cool hand on my fevered brow. I cuddled in her embrace.

After my prayer, I meditated on those who would read this book, which has in no way been a how-to book but rather an encouragement for each person to find his or her own way. And yet it seemed that the Holy Spirit was asking me to share a little of the how-to of this particular journey of mine, a journey that continues. Over the days that followed, I felt better and stronger.

After a rejection, when you are seeking to heal you heart and forgive

- Share your hurt with an accepting and trusted friend, if possible. Don't choose anyone who will fuss at you or instruct you. The important thing is to get your thoughts out in a safe place. Depending on your priest's or minister's personality and style, he or she may be able to help you.

- Seek prayer and healing rituals. Create as beautiful a space as you can, and visit it daily. Use any form of prayer that works for you, but pray specifically about your problem.

- Avoid punishing yourself. Be gentle with yourself. Get a massage if you can, or go see a happy movie. Read uplifting material, or paint a picture. Often, when bad things happen to us, we subconsciously believe that we deserve them; then we add to our misery by being unkind and by depriving ourselves. This is the time we most need to practice healthy self-love.

- Ask forgiveness from God, and forgive yourself for your faults. Resolve to learn from the hurtful situation.

- Release your anger. Write angry letters. (Don't send them! Tear them up.) Exercise. I am very fortunate that I get to go to a pool. Walking is also an excellent way to dispel depression and anger. You can also put on music and dance.

- Journal in depth about your feelings.

- Give yourself the gift of time to heal. Be patient with your own ups and downs. Realize that all interior change takes time. But time really does heal!

You can repeat all of these practices as often as needed. In fact, most are helpful whether we are in desolation or not. Most important, as you resume your everyday chores and routine, try to avoid focusing on any hurtful incident. Practice gratitude instead. Let go.

Ignatius knew that one who is unwilling to bear affronts to pride would lack the spiritual muscle to run the long race of service to Christ. But his attitudes must be looked at in the context of his worldview. He wanted his comrades in faith to know that, compared to the great length, depth, and richness of God's love, the slights of the world did not matter. It is an attitude we can all seek to adopt, and yet we must deal with our feelings as they are now.

I haven't developed such spiritual muscle that large slights are easily forgotten, but I am trying. For me, it would indeed be a great grace to reach that sort of surrender. Until then, I pray that God will give me the strength to love myself in all my imperfection.

For Journaling and Reflection

❧ What is your initial response to the steps listed for healing after a rejection or disappointment? Write about how you might pursue these steps if needed.

❧ List some ways in which you are kind to yourself. Write about how you can become even more kind.

❧ Do you have a special place to pray? If so, describe it. If not, write about the place you might create just for prayer.

27

Unbelievable Forgiveness

The Second Point: I will listen to what the persons on the face of the earth are saying; that is, how they speak with one another, swear and blaspheme, and so on. Likewise, I will hear what the Divine Persons are saying, that is, "Let us work the redemption of the human race."

IGNATIUS OF LOYOLA, *The Spiritual Exercises*

"Lord, how often must I forgive my brother if he wrongs me? As often as seven times?" Jesus answered, "Not seven, I tell you, but seventy-seven times."

MATTHEW 18:21–22

I am about to write a story of unbelievable forgiveness now. It is based upon facts; I have fictionalized some details in order to protect the privacy of the people involved. You may not believe it; it may astonish or even sicken you. After hearing the story, you may think, *Why should anyone forgive this much?* The story is true, and that is what gives me the courage to write it. The main character of this story is a better person that I am, and she exemplifies the type of radical forgiveness that Christ told his disciples about.

Rosemary's heart was heavy in many ways: Her husband had been out of work for several months and did not seem to be trying hard to find a new job. Their relationship was suffering, and Rosemary prayed daily about it, asking the Lord to heal their lives. She was devout in her faith, and it gave her great comfort. She always believed that the Lord had a plan for her life and that he would move her through her difficulties.

As she pulled into traffic, Rosemary pushed a rosary tape into the cassette deck and the gentle sounds of the prayer filled her car. She prayed softly with the tape, "Hail, Mary, full of grace, the Lord is with you. . . ."

Rosemary sped up just a bit. She didn't want to be late; she needed this job since it was their only income. Finding a parking place, she hurried in to her desk and found a stack of folders for her to process. "Not even time for a cup of coffee." She sighed as she picked up the first folder and began to add and check numbers.

About an hour later, Rosemary felt nauseated. She rose from her desk and went to the rest room where she pressed a cold, wet paper towel to her forehead. Her supervisor entered the restroom.

"Rosemary! You are sick! You're white as a ghost. Go home; we'll cover for you."

Reluctantly, Rosemary agreed that she was probably catching the flu and shouldn't risk giving it to others. She got in her car and drove slowly home.

Rosemary smiled a little, even through her nausea, as she entered her subdivision. The neat homes in her area gave her a sense of comfort. She and Dave had been there for many years, and they were friendly with many of their neighbors. She continued down the leafy street and pulled into her driveway. As she entered, she saw that a blue Buick with a University of Louisiana bumper sticker was parked in her driveway.

That's funny, she thought. *That looks like Lenore's car. I wonder what she's doing here.* Feeling every degree of her mounting fever, Rosemary entered her home calling, "Dave? Where are you? I was sick and had to come home."

Her stomach lurched as she heard scrambling in the back of her home—in their bedroom. The living room began to spin, and Rosemary rushed to the toilet and threw up. Around her, doors were slamming, and the blue Buick spun out of her driveway.

She sat down on her couch shakily and began to cry. She also began to pray: "Lord, I know you will help me to face every challenge. I know you are here with me now. And I know you said that if I don't forgive I will not be forgiven. I forgive them, Lord. Help me! Oh, Lord, help me!"

Her husband, Dave, was as pale as she had been when he finally entered the living room. "Rosemary. Oh, my God. I've been feeling so bad about not working and—" His voice trailed off. They both knew no excuse was good enough.

Rosemary lifted her head and met his eyes. "I forgive you," she said. "And I forgive Lenore. I want Lenore to come here, and I want us to pray together. We must meet this all with prayer."

I will leave the story there. Rosemary's cousin told me that the three actually did pray together. I have to chuckle a little at how uncomfortable Dave and Lenore must have been. I don't understand how Rosemary could forgive so quickly. As the months and years passed, it was clear to all around her that this forgiveness was not an act or a denial. She had truly forgiven, and she treated both her husband and her neighbor Lenore with kindness.

This path is not for everyone. I almost didn't write this story because I didn't even know if Rosemary was wise or sane! Yet she has shown, as time has passed, that she chose the best path for her. So few have the faith to live this radical forgiveness that it is indeed surprising when a person actually does it.

There is a telling, amusing story of Ignatius, after his conversion, intercepting his brother's mistress at the door and sending her away. One can almost see him, standing in for Jesus, saying to the surprised lady, "Go and sin no more." Although Ignatius had what approached a horror for sin, he had no horror of sinners. As Jesus did, Ignatius embraced them, taught them, and loved them. For me, the sin of Dave and Lenore was not sex; it was betrayal. It was a failure of love, and yet I know without a doubt that Ignatius would have approved of Rosemary's radical forgiveness.

For Journaling and Reflection

✿ Think about times when you have had to forgive others. Write about the incident that is most memorable for you.

✿ How do you feel about Rosemary's forgiveness? How does it compare to the Lord's command to his apostles? Is it unrealistic for you? Why or why not?

❄ In what ways can you move toward being a more forgiving person? If there is a specific person you need to forgive, how can you move toward doing so?

❄ Write about anything for which you need to forgive yourself.

28

Grayson, Child of Loss

How can the providence of God permit the sufferings of humanity in this world? We need to approach it as a mystery rather than a problem. Our limited humanity is constantly going through change. . . . [T]he relationship between suffering and our sins, our disorder, and our moral imperfections . . . does not imply that individuals necessarily cause their own physical suffering by their own sins. Yet, the totality of evil perpetrated by the human race has somehow brought about physical suffering, even for the innocent.

JOHN J. ENGLISH, S.J., *Spiritual Freedom*

The world is a desperate place. I see it in the faces of the abused and neglected who come for therapy and write or call for spiritual support. And I encounter it on a daily basis in the broader arena of today's news reports as well.

ROBERT J. WICKS, *Seeds of Sensitivity*

I sat in my speech-therapy office at the local elementary school, flipping through a report. A little boy knocked shyly on the door. "Come in, honey," I said. "Close the door behind you."

Grayson was a new first-grade student, seven years old, who had transferred to the school. He had a speech-therapy evaluation that qualified him for my services, and I was meeting him for the first time. I smiled because I had been taught thirty years ago that this first session was to "establish rapport," and I never failed to remember that phrase.

"Grayson," I said in my most rapportly voice, "tell me about your family. How many brothers and sisters do you have?" I looked kindly at the little fellow. Grayson was extremely neat and clean, in a navy short-sleeved shirt and khaki shorts. He had soft brown curls and dark expressive eyes.

There was a short silence; then Grayson looked up at me with his liquid eyes. "My baby died," he said.

"Oh, I am so sorry! A little baby died?"

"My daddy killed it. It was my daddy, not the baby's daddy."

I sat frozen in my chair. This information was not in Grayson's file. Could he be confused? Maybe television? Of course not! Obviously a baby had died.

"Sweetie," I whispered, "what do you mean your daddy killed the baby?"

"Well, my mama was at choir practice, and he was baby-sitting us, and he threw the baby. The baby was crying and crying, and I said, 'No, Daddy,' and Mama came home and she was screaming, 'Not my baby, not my baby. You killed my baby.' "

All this information came flowing out in a smooth torrent, with appropriate changes of inflection and volume. What did I do now?

"Grayson, this is all so sad. I am so sorry this happened. I'm going to see if Miss Moss is busy, and would you mind telling her the story?"

"No, ma'am." A pause. "I cry a lot at night."

I put my hand on his head. "Yes, I can understand why, Grayson. Okay. Go back to class, and I will get you in a little bit."

I knocked on the principal's door and then entered. "Mary," I said, "do you know that new little boy Grayson?" She nodded.

"Well, he says that his daddy killed his baby brother while his mother was at choir practice—" I had to stop for a moment because tears had caught my voice. I had heard too many sad stories from little children lately, and it was beginning to seem unbearable. "We need to know what's going on with him. His problems may be mostly emotional."

"Well, I hadn't heard about this," said Mary. "He comes from another parish, and it would be a little hard to track this down, but maybe we can make a home visit."

Later that week, after Grayson had told the principal the story, we sat in the family's living room, talking with his mother and grandmother. His grandmother was holding a picture of the little baby, Toby, who had died. "He was nine months," said the grandmother. "That was a fine, fat baby, nothing wrong with him at all."

"One Wednesday night last May, I had gone to the church for practice," said Grayson's mother, "and Grayson's daddy, Joe, was there and supposed to watch the children, and the baby was crying. And I guess he couldn't take it or something, and he threw Toby. It hurt his head. I always said, just leave the baby in the bed if it makes you nervous! But he stopped breathing, and then Joe tried to wrap him up and say he was sick, but that baby wasn't ever sick."

"Can I see?" I said. I took the picture of the smiling infant in my hands. He was dressed in a blue and white sailor outfit. Baby fat creased on his strong little legs, and light shone in his eyes. His head was covered with thick brown curls like Grayson's.

"It's just a terrible thing," I said. "Where is Grayson's daddy now?"

"In jail. He's not getting out, either."

For some reason, I felt only a little better hearing his. The damage was done to every member of this family, and nothing would change that now.

We talked a little about Grayson seeing the counselor at school. We left in sadness.

The school principal has a close relationship to the Lafayette Carmelite nuns, and she often sends a "lamp of love" from them. This means that the sisters will pray specifically for the person for whom the lamp of love is sent and burn a special candle for three days. The recipients also receive a beautiful card. We sent one for Grayson's family, for Toby, and his mother and grand-mother. So little solace for their great suffering. I hope it helped a little.

I was as kind to Grayson as I could be, but he and his family didn't stay long in our area. The neighborhood into which they had moved was crime-laden, and they returned to the rural parish they were from. I haven't thought about them for a long time, yet a lump has risen in my throat. I can see the picture of that baby clearly in my mind's eye. I prayed for the family as I remembered them.

And what about Joe? How could he have done such a thing? Did a moment's uncontrolled anger lead to tragedy? Was he an alcoholic? Mentally ill? How much did grinding poverty play a part in this drama? Did Joe ever ask for forgiveness from God, or from his ex-wife? From his son, Grayson? Why did the baby's mother leave the baby with him in the first place? Was she aware of any risk? I don't have the answers to any of these questions. And I know that in homes across the world, similar questions are repeated daily. As my friend Sister Bea Doueren says, "What is life-giving? What is leading to death? This is the way we can know what sin is."

What is hardest to believe is that all Joe has to do is ask for God's forgiveness and it will be given. In my hardness of heart, I would like for it to be much harder than this, but then being in prison for life is also a tragedy. Joe is paying the price. Yet even in prison, he is not shut away from our God of welcoming and redeeming love.

I remembered that Joe was once someone's nine-month old. Was he loved? Was he abused? When did the violence begin, and how is violence stopped? When did Joe start on the road that led to death? These questions echo through the years as I remember Grayson, Toby, and their family.

Grayson's story is not an isolated case. I have experienced sorrow and fear while watching the news lately. In Baton Rouge, there seems to be a serial killer on the loose. Many young women have been killed recently in this area. In other states, children have been snatched from their homes or yards and murdered. The devastating effects of child abuse are also reported almost daily. As a Christian, I am charged with having my eyes open and not numbing myself to the problems of the world. At the same time, I must not fall into despair. In order to avoid growing small and isolated in my fear, I want to continue to follow that which is life-giving.

Ignatius saw terrible problems as he worked with the poor and rich alike. He was well acquainted with the problems and passions of the human race. Not long after his conversion, he had considered entering a monastery. I wonder if sometimes he longed for the quiet life of prayer he would have found there.

Yet, in his hard-won humility, Ignatius did not separate himself from a fallen and sinful world, in part because he perceived himself to be one of its greatest sinners, now restored by God's love. He continued to tell others about this life of faith. No one he encountered was excluded from the kingdom or beyond the graced touch of God's help.

And so I invite us all to say, as we examine our own hearts, "What is leading to life? What is making me larger and more loving? This is the way I must go."

I close my eyes and I see Grayson. He is a happy little boy now, playing outside, running with his friends around the playground as the dark memories of the past fade. Well, this is my hope. He has a mother and grandmother who love him dearly and care for him well. I hope this is enough. I hope he can have a childhood that is filled with fun and joy and treats, and much love.

For Journaling and Reflection

❧ Do you feel that God easily forgives all sin? Explain.

❧ Describe how your capacity for forgiveness has either increased or decreased along your life's path.

❧ What actions on your part lead you to greater life? What can lead you into darkness?

❧ How do you process the news of tragedy and sin in our world? How does it affect your prayer life?

29

Humility

The enemy tries his second weapon: pride and vainglory. He tells the person that he possesses much goodness and holiness, and exalts him higher than he deserves.

IGNATIUS OF LOYOLA, IN A LETTER TO TERESA REJADELL

Anyone who is wise or understanding among you should from a good life give evidence of deeds done in the gentleness of wisdom. But if at heart you have bitterness of jealousy, or selfish ambition, do not be boastful or hide the truth with lies; this is not the wisdom that comes from above.

JAMES 3:13–15

*I*t is difficult for those of us who have struggled with low self-esteem to understand what true humility might be. True humility is seeing ourselves as we truly are, neither overstating our achievements nor underestimating our gifts.

Humility involves leading the lives we are given to the best of our ability, being who we are now, where we are now. This journey requires a careful sifting and separating of the desires of the heart and the demands of the ego. It also requires us to claim our worth, our heritage as children of Christ's kingdom. We have been given many gifts, and we need to celebrate them.

Do you remember Kathleen from chapter 25? She wrote these words:

Where one blooms is where one dies,
So to turn this ground, here where one is,
Requires the humility and courage of farming.
Not counting on the harvest while plowing.
Risking the shock of a late freeze
that melts the tapered buds of Spring;
wax petals dripping from trees.

Planted, one endures, and dwells.

We must die to ego so that the One who planted us will bloom in us. This is the Christ within. St. Ignatius knew this; he was burned in the cleansing frost of love. He was struck down in battle, something that might have been deemed a great misfortune, yet it was the turning point of his amazing life. In his bed of pain, he began to be the man God wanted. He commenced to leave aside his vainglory and pride; as his heart changed, his feet turned in an entirely new direction.

It is important that we see our worth. We are good and we are worthy; Jesus died teaching this. And we are creatures of the Creator. We cannot artificially increase ourselves to great size. We must be "planted." And we must "endure and dwell" under the hand of the farmer.

As Kathleen's poem continues:

Something in being rooted; about turning
and composting a small, personal plot
causes me to ask, if not happy now, then when?

In the field, light electric on the cane, I see
The indestructible bones of the Farmer,
crooking his finger at me.

(I cannot)
Maintain myself in seed,
Going from winter to winter,
Avoiding Spring and the telling fruit. . . .
the only way out, is through. . . .

This morning the sun rose blood-red, casting sharp rays of color through my stained-glass bedroom window. I pulled the patch-work quilt around my shoulders against the early morning chill. For a moment, I cherished all of life's lessons: painful and joyful.

Life is this patchwork of the humble and the radiant. We may try to avoid life, staying in bed, refusing to bloom, so that we may avoid our failures, our heartbreaks. But this ground of the heart is the ground we must cultivate. This, then, is the ground where we stand. Only rooted in God's love do I have the courage to be humble.

For Journaling and Reflection

❦ How do humility or pride manifest themselves in your life? (Remember that low self-esteem is not humility.)

❦ Describe how illness or loss has increased your humility—or not. Perhaps such struggles have made you more resistant or angry. Write and/or pray about all of what you are feeling as you consider this.

❦ Reread Kathleen's poem. How could it apply to your life? What parts of yourself (perhaps your deepest feelings?) are you afraid to cultivate and to share with others? What is the nature of your personal "garden plot"?

❦ Who can you trust enough to talk with about your more private thoughts and feelings? Write about that person.

30

The Direction of the Heart

[I] ask for growing and intense sorrows and tears for my sins.
IGNATIUS OF LOYOLA, *The Spiritual Exercises*

[I] ask for an interior knowledge of our Lord, who became human for me, that I may love him more intensely and follow him more closely.
IGNATIUS OF LOYOLA, *The Spiritual Exercises*

I walked with 125 singers, dressed in black and white, who filed onto the altar at Our Lady of Fatima Church in Lafayette. My heart was beating quickly as I took my place with the altos, and I wondered if our intense rehearsals would come fully to fruition. So much had happened so fast, musically speaking, and our sheet music was filled with pencil notes and frantic reminders.

The first several songs went well, and I realized that all I needed to do was tune in to our conductor, Christopher Walker. I knew the music well enough. Then we sang a short Celtic prayer, recently put to music by Christopher:

Heart of my own heart,
Whatever may befall me.
Rule over my thoughts, my feelings, my words.

Heart of my own heart,
Whatever may befall me,
Be with me, in all that I do.

©2000, Christopher Walker. Published by OCP Publications, 5536 NE Hassalo, Portland OR 97213. All rights reserved. Used with permission.

As the flute soared and trembled and the harmonies rose, I saw that Christopher's eyes were filled with tears. I was having no trouble putting feeling into the words of the song. And I wondered, *What was this "Heart of my own heart"?*

Upon reflection, I chose to believe that we were singing of the Holy Spirit, that divine part of us that is the center of our own hearts. The Holy Spirit who, upon receiving an invitation, will guide our feelings, our words, and be with us in all that we do.

How many times have I struggled with "my feelings, my words"? Too many. How many times have I said the wrong thing, hurt someone, taken offense, been sarcastic, or distanced myself? Yet I can't expect to reach perfection even if I knew what perfection is!

How wonderful that we are always welcomed back by the loving, forgiving Spirit. We are welcomed with open arms by the Father/Mother God who exults in our very humanness, by the God who understands. This is the God of whom Jesus spoke, the Father who welcomed back the Prodigal Son with an open, generous heart. Here is a God who desires not to punish but to redeem.

It is this knowledge of the nature of the triune God that gives me the courage to follow God more closely. Ignatius always counseled his spiritual directees to ask for what they desired. I desire to grow to be more like this forgiving God. It's a long journey, and I may not complete it.

Years ago, I attended a retreat hosted by a dynamic woman named Mary Margaret, who was a sister (I don't remember her order). She advised us, "Don't be dismayed about the fact that Jesus said, 'Be perfect as my Father is perfect.'" The word Jesus used for "perfect" was *telios,* and it conveys the meaning of being pointed in a direction. She told us, "When you miss the mark, just keep picking yourself up and pointing yourself in the right direction again!"

Her words have given me tremendous comfort. It is the direction of our heart that matters, much more so than our mistakes.

In his book *Letting God Come Close,* William Barry states, "What was the original genial insight of Ignatius of Loyola? I would say that it was the idea that God can be found in all things, that every human experience has a religious dimension and religious meaning." So, we pray, "Be with me in all that I do."

I will follow my director, St. Ignatius. I think I am beginning to know the words to the song, and so I sing, "Heart of my own heart, let me see you in all things. Let me forgive myself, and let me point myself daily in the direction of loving kindness and forgiveness for others."

For Journaling and Reflection

❧ Look back over your journaling with previous chapters if you wish. What insights have you gained about sin and forgiveness? Respond to these insights in writing and in prayer.

PRAYER TO THE GOD
WHO FORGIVES

God, you brought life out of nothingness and chaos,
I believe you are still doing this today.
Move in my spirit,
and calm my disordered thinking,
my wayward, selfish heart.

I believe in your patient and forgiving love,
even when I am tempted to despair,
by the darkness that is all around
and within me.

Let us start over again, God.
Let your light pour in, clean and bright!
I put my hand in yours.
I resolve to develop my strengths, as I walk with you;
to meet each dawn with hope,
to daily grow in love.

31

A Tiny Girl Gets Better

Now it remains for me to ask you, for the service of God our Lord, to assist us with your good works and prayers in a project we have undertaken for God's glory. . . . I pray to his Divine Majesty to dispose of us and of everyone in the way we may best serve him in all things and in all things give thanks for ever and ever.

IGNATIUS OF LOYOLA, IN A LETTER TO
MAGDALENA DE LOYOLA Y ARROZ

*M*y sister Judy held the phone in her hand and took a deep breath. "So, you think they will need to stay a full twelve months?" she said to the nurse at the Shriners' hospital.

"Oh, yes," the nurse replied. "There will be intake summaries, evaluations, and then if and when she has the surgery, there will be months of rehabilitation."

My sister hung up the phone in trepidation. "Lord," she prayed, "I know you are calling me to do this. But a whole year with a woman I don't know well, and an ill two-year-old in my home! I'm really worried that I am not up to this challenge."

My sister is one of the world's unsung heroes. She is always giving to others, and she often has people, usually exchange students, living with her and her husband, Hall. Her daughter and son-in-law, Lara and Milton, are missionaries in Lithuania, and their friends needed help. The little girl, Gintare, was born with osteogenesis imperfecta, a sort of brittle-bone disease, and her devoted single mother, Laima, was trying to get medical help for her in the United States. Gintare's father had quickly left when she was born; he wanted no part of raising a disabled child. Laima tried to make ends meet with a small stipend from the state and odd jobs, as she cared for her daughter. Gintare was two and a half years old and had never walked. She had had surgery in Lithuania with bad results. She was an unhappy, unhealthy little child.

Laima met Lara and Milton in Lithuania and joined their church. Soon the couple prayed about how they could help this family. In June 1999, my sister Judy traveled to Lithuania with a Shriner's application in hand. After some time, the Shriners accepted the case. Friends, clubs, and church members in Lithuania helped to fund the trip to America. And that's when my sister found out that she would have houseguests for a whole year.

During that same year, Judy and Hall were hosting a Chinese exchange student, Amy, and there were problems. Judy told me on the telephone, "Amy is not fitting into our family very well. She sometimes makes herself ill studying all night. She's a perfectionist about schoolwork, and we can't get her to have a perspective on it. She also stays on the computer way too much."

My sister worried about how the addition of a fragile child and her mother would work out, along with this other stress. Like me, Judy loves peace and quiet, time to read, and freedom to pursue her interests and run her home as she likes. But she was willing to make this sacrifice, and God had plans for it, it seems.

After she arrived at Judy and Hall's home, Gintare charmed everyone she met. Although she couldn't get around very much, she exhibited wonderful intelligence on her elfin face. Her health began to improve right away, with a balanced diet and vitamins. Her green eyes began to sparkle, and her blonde hair got thicker and shinier. Laima was a wonderful addition to the household, and, without being asked, she helped Judy clean, cook, and weed the vegetable garden. Laima was so touched by every generosity shown to her. She was a determined woman. She strove to improve her English and to understand the treatments that her daughter would undergo. Even Amy, the exchange student, began to be more sociable when little Gintare made her entrance.

One day during this year, I was visiting my sister, and Gintare was playing with the remote control. "She loves to play with it," said Judy, "but she can't really make it work." All at once, Gintare pressed a button and the TV picture dissolved to snow and loud buzzing. There was a shocked look on the two year old's face. Then she quickly put down the remote control and picked up a gardening brochure, appearing to be lost in thought as she flipped through it. The unspoken message was clear: "Don't blame me, I had nothing to do with it." I laughed until I cried. The tiny, feisty child was winning my heart as she did everyone else's.

More people than can be named contributed money and time to help Gintare and Laima. The day came for the operation. Church members gave blood in case Gintare needed it. The operation was a success, but she was encased in a body cast with just an opening for her diaper. She had to remain in a prone position for six weeks. This was a long and trying time for everyone involved. Some of the procedures Gintare had to endure made Judy cry.

Once they were home, Judy taped a large piece of paper to the refrigerator door for Gintare to draw on. She drew and colored for hours. Laima devoted herself to her daughter's care as everyone prayed for a good final outcome.

When the cast was removed, a carpenter friend, Bill, made a standing frame according to doctor's directions. Gintare was fitted with braces. Laima learned how to be her daughter's physical therapist. Then one day it happened. Gintare walked! She walked with her braces and a tiny walker. As Laima and Judy cried, Gintare walked into her future. A future crafted by God's hand.

Close your eyes now. See a cozy new church in a little village in Lithuania. See the front doors open. See a young mother named Laima, dressed in a new blue dress, gently wiping her tears. See a diminutive child named Gintare, a tiny blonde sprite of a child, who had left this very same church a year before lying helpless in a sort of a cradle. See her walk now, slowly down the aisle, and you will see everyone in the church rise and applaud. For now, their prayers have been answered.

Ignatius of Loyola performed his healing work on earth, dispensing aid to those who needed it. He did not stand aloof from the poor but lived among them and lived as they did, adopting a rough sacking garment and begging for his food. What made this so impressive was the luxury and prestige he had enjoyed earlier in life.

In one memorable incident during his conversion years, he gave away everything he had to other beggars who found him in a church. He apologized to them when he had given his last penny away! Ignatius lived in hostels and shared the table with the needy, following Jesus' example of loving the poor and respecting those on the margins of society—people such as Laima and Gintare, who are blessings themselves. For now, Judy says, "A task that was begun most reluctantly has become one of the greatest blessings of my life."

For Journaling and Reflection

❧ What form of service are you called to? Describe how you are participating in this service now or how you plan to participate in the future.

❧ How do you react to people who are physically or mentally challenged? What do you feel is God's role in their lives?

❧ Would you have had the courage to do what Judy did? Why or why not? What other things do you want to do, for which you need more courage?

❧ Describe how helping others has affected your life.

32

Compassion Shared

If you deprive yourself for the hungry
and satisfy the needs of the afflicted,
your light will rise in the darkness,
and your darkest hour will be like noon.
Yahweh will always guide you,
will satisfy your needs in the scorched land;
he will give strength to your bones
and you will be like a watered garden,
like a flowing spring
whose waters never run dry.

ISAIAH 58:10–11

After my mystical experience in Chimayo, I met my husband in the beautiful old Spanish town of Santa Fe. We stayed on the square in one of the oldest hotels, and it was so good to be with him after our time apart.

He agreed to come with me back to Chimayo to revisit the place of my experience. Really, I couldn't put a lot of that experience into words. I just told him that it was a beautiful little village and filled with interesting sights.

We traveled the poorly marked roads and entered the town and toured the church. We sat in the shaded courtyard and ate our snacks. With my notoriously poor sense of direction, I hoped that I could find again the spot of my vision. It wasn't difficult, as we followed the sound of the rushing water. The same black dog that had greeted me previously wagged his body at me once more. We walked through private yards, and again, the tolerant people living there just nodded cordially to us. The smell of cooking onions and beans drifted from one of the homes, and we heard voices raised in rapid conversation over the drone of a television.

I was once again filled with a sense of wonder as we approached the clear, moving water. Several rather thin steers and cows nudged at a fence to the right of the path. I looked in idle amusement as Dee picked up an empty plastic milk jug on the ground, took out his pocketknife, and cut the top off of it. He walked to the stream, rinsed the jug, and filled it with water.

He doesn't know what a holy place this is for me, I thought. *He's just fooling around.* I admit it, I felt smug in the aftermath of my "oneness" experience. I thought that my husband couldn't really understand this special place.

As I watched, Dee poured the water into the trough in front of the thin animals. They began to drink at once, clearly very thirsty and relieved to get the water. Dee refilled the plastic container many times and filled the trough

"Now, fellows," he said. "Now you feel better."

To say I was humbled was to put it mildly. As Fr. Richard Rohr says, "I am glad that Jesus has come into your life, but what does it mean that he has come?" Are we kinder? Are we more sensitive to the needs of others? Are we less judgmental? Does our sense of oneness with all cause us to realize that we are cocreators with God; does it cause us to contribute to the quality of life on this earth?

Ignatius wrote in depth about humility and service. For him, this humility was wrapped in gratitude. He says, "Why have the angels, though they are the sword of God's justice, tolerated me, guarded me, and prayed for me? Why have the saints interceded for me and asked favors for me? And the heavens, sun, moon, stars, and the elements: the fruits, birds, fishes, and other animals, why have they all been at my service?" (quoted in *Spiritual Freedom* by John J. English, S.J.)

If my sin at the river was the sin of pride, then as English states, "The only antidote to sin is the compassion of God, the kindness of God." And only through humbly feeling and accepting this compassion and tenderness can we bring it to those people and creatures around us.

For Journaling and Reflection

✻ How has an experience of your own suffering or healing changed the way you treat others who are suffering?

✻ What people do you admire for their kindness?

✤ Describe any animals in your life, whether pets you tend or wild creatures you observe. What has been the effect of these creatures upon your life?

33

Portrait of a Mother Who Loved Well

[Mary] stored up all these things in her heart.

LUKE 2:51

*I*melda loved to talk about her garden. She would say, "My cucumbers are going good, but my tomatoes didn't do a thing!" Her daughter Linda would laugh and say, "Yeah, I guess we better get out the pickle jars. She's got a million cucumbers!"

Imelda was the matriarch of a large clan. The family lived in what they laughingly called "Trailer City," on several acres in the country. Linda, her husband and grown children, various spouses, and her sister Joan lived near Imelda in a series of mobile homes. Joan, who was younger than Linda, suffered severely from cancer, and everyone did what they could to help her and her children. There was so much family living so close, I confided to Linda that I didn't think I could handle living like that! Yet, I admired their tightly knit family.

Imelda sang in the St. Joseph Choir. She took her place in the back row and sang and giggled with the other "older ladies." She encouraged Linda, a talented soloist, to keep singing.

Everything changed one day when Imelda suffered a severe stroke. One day she was gardening and singing, the next, she was struck down. Months of nursing led eventually to a peaceful death.

We were told to wear red to the funeral. It was Imelda's favorite color, and we were going to celebrate her life. I was about to learn much more about that life.

At the end of the service, Imelda's son and his wife approached the podium. His wife was there to give moral support. She glanced lovingly at her husband as he began to speak.

"My mother provided us all with words of wisdom. And she did it under the most trying of circumstances. My father taught by his absence; he taught me that I didn't want to be like him. My mother taught by her constant service.

"We were five kids. Try to imagine, if you can, no car, no phone, no television. My mom walked up on the levee and caught a ride to work every day for twenty years. She worked at St. Aloysius Elementary School in the cafeteria."

He chuckled. "Guys, I can still remember those peanut butter cookies she brought home on Thursdays. Were they good! She could make a penny walk, man! She could feed five hungry kids with little or nothing. Sometimes her brothers would come over and fix things. Everything in our house got fixed, not replaced. And that garden she had! It went on for miles! I have eaten vegetables that you have never even heard of—and hoed around them, too."

He smiled. "And she encouraged us to get our education, to have more and to be more. Oh, she could get mad at us, sure.

And sometimes we got off track and really tried her patience. But we never, never doubted her love for us."

He looked up. "Now, I don't want to paint too dark a picture. Sometimes Mom had fun. She loved to dance. And she would get ready early, wearing red, and her sister would pick her up. I can still see her sitting in the front room, waiting for her ride to the dance. She would be so excited. But we never met her dance partners. No, Mom came home again by eleven and lived just for us. That was her choice.

"Mom was deeply religious. She led us in the rosary and made sure that we got to Mass. I am sure her faith got her through many a lonely time.

"For us kids, Mom was the answer for so long. She was the heart of our family. And I guess she still is. Enjoy heaven, Mom." The handsome, articulate son of Imelda, Allen, took his wife's hand and walked sadly and proudly back to his seat.

As we stated earlier, St. Ignatius probably lost his mother when he was very young. Other women, however, nurtured him and helped him in his ministry. Primarily, he was devoted to the Virgin Mary, and early on he left his sword and shield at her feet. He always eagerly sought her intercession.

St. Ignatius, Imelda, and Mother Mary—how are they alike? They were immersed bodily, day by day, in the work that was set before them. For the great saint, it was helping the poor as he lived among them, and forming the Jesuit Society from the inside out. Mother Mary must have struggled to understand her role, that of the Savior's mother. Hers were the hands that washed his face, fixed his meals, and cradled his body as it descended from the cross.

Feisty Imelda accepted the job of raising five children without a partner, with all that this entailed. She could have bailed out, saying, "It's too hard to do this alone." Or she could have turned to drugs or alcohol to ease the heart that must have often been lonely. She didn't take any of these roads. She made the best of it, with peanut butter cookies, a red dress, and vegetables you never heard of. She even knew the joy of the dance.

For Journaling and Reflection

❧ What simple forms of service lie at your fingertips every day?

❧ Who serves you in simple yet profound ways? Is there an "Imelda" in your life?

❧ How are your roles in your family changing and/or growing?

❧ What parts of family life and service are most difficult for you? What are the easiest and most rewarding parts?

34

Abbigail's Heart of Service

Images have the power to move the heart and bring about transformation. . . . Like music they reach into the deepest part of our being and change us, giving us insight and releasing energy.

JOHN J. ENGLISH, S.J., *Spiritual Freedom*

For it is not much knowledge that fills and satisfies the soul, but the intimate understanding and relishing of the truth.

IGNATIUS OF LOYOLA, *The Spiritual Exercises*

While Abbigail was on mission in Haiti, she began to collect heart-shaped stones. They seemed to be everywhere, worn smooth in old creek beds or along the dusty roads.

When she arrived home with the heart symbols, she felt inspired to begin giving them to those in pain or trouble. Abbigail felt that these little rocks were holy; they were holy at least for her. They had come from a place that held her deepest, most profound experiences of God.

One Saturday morning, while I was washing clothes, Abbigail called me. We discussed her healing story. Then Abbigail began to tell me about one of her experiences with the heart-shaped stones.

Abbigail and her husband have three children: a son, Adam, who is nineteen, and two daughters, eighteen and twelve. Abbigail's story was about Adam.

"I was going to the hospital, and my heart was heavy about him. He was quitting college, and I feared he wouldn't go back. I was praying so hard that he wouldn't quit.

"My friend Justine and I were there to see a lady who was about to undergo heart surgery, and she wasn't well at all. It was a serious situation. We chatted with her and prayed together. I recalled that I had a cream-colored heart stone with me. I gave her the little stone and told her I hoped it would bring God's love and his healing a little closer to her. I also asked her to pray for my son. I explained my worries about him, not only his quitting college but about his future and his happiness.

"She looked into my eyes; I will never forget this. Here was a woman who by all rights should have been completely tuned in to her own fear and pain, but she comforted me! She said, 'Honey, your son will return to school.'

"I don't know how she had such insight. But I knew she was correct. My heart warmed and I felt such comfort."

As usual, I was transfixed by Abbigail's stories. The swoosh, swoosh of the washing machine brought me back to the present. I pressed the receiver to my ear. "Abbigail, was that lady all right after her surgery?"

"Yes, she was. She came through just fine, and her health improved." She paused. "And the very next semester, Adam returned to school."

Last night, I meditated on this story of Abbigail's son. In my mind's eye, I could see how healing love and service circulate through God's people: from God's heart to ours, out to others, and returning to us again to continue the cycle. All we have to do is cooperate with the flow of that healing love. As the famous prayer attributed to St. Francis of Assisi tells us, "It is in giving that we receive."

In Abbigail's initial service in Haiti, she found a means to continue bringing a little touch of comfort to those around her in her hometown. And through that giving, she receives. Because she receives, it is easier for her to continue the cycle of giving, of loving. She has found the image of the heart, which "like music, reaches the deepest part of our being."

St. Ignatius of Loyola was called into a life of great service. In establishing the Jesuit Society, he began a movement with strong, worldwide influences for good. It was not easy for him. He battled with poor health, with suspicions on the part of the church (even imprisonment), and with some relationships that, far from being nourishing, were sometimes embarrassing and painful. He persevered because of his sure knowledge of God's love for him: "the intimate understanding and relishing of the truth." And because he relished this truth, he dedicated himself totally to love and the service of God, despite its price. Because of God's spirit in him, and his cooperation with it, so many serve others today, four hundred years later. Ignatius's voice still speaks to us. I even dare to hope that he speaks in some small way through these lines that I write.

For Journaling and Reflection

❦ What gifts or skills do you share with others?

❦ What form of service helps you to bring God's love to others?

❦ Who encourages and nourishes you in your service or work?

❦ In what way do you receive when you are giving? Or, do you give too much?

❦ Write about any concerns you have about choices made by members of your family.

35

Serving Others in Our Weakness

To Yahweh when I am in trouble
I call and he answers me.

PSALM 120:1

Whoever wishes to come with me must labor with me, so that
through following me in the pain he or she may follow me also
in the glory.

IGNATIUS OF LOYOLA, *The Spiritual Exercises*

*M*y sister's friend Cathy has suffered much in her young life. Cathy lost two sisters during her childhood to autoimmune disorders. One lived only a short time, but one was in and out of hospitals for years, causing Cathy the stress of watching a sister die. She often had to stay with friends as her mother and father were estranged. Her mother was at the hospital most of the time with her sister, and her father was not around much when she was growing up. He is now very supportive and is kind and helpful to her and her children. She also lost a brother at birth from hyaline membrane disease: immature lungs.

Then, when Cathy was in her very early twenties, her mother, who had remarried some years earlier, died of cancer. After her mother died, Cathy was left with a ten-year-old brother to raise, as his father had died of cancer several years before. When Cathy discovered she had ovarian cancer just before her wedding, Chris, her fiancé, knew he was marrying a woman with cancer who had a ten-year-old brother to raise. He married her with no hesitation.

My sister Minnett recently wrote to me. "I got to know Cathy through a mutual friend of her deceased mother, Carolyn DeHondt. This was when Cathy was planning her wedding, before she discovered the cancer. I became one of what we call her ''Nother Mothers' and helped her plan her wedding; I was the mother of the bride in many ways. When the cancer halted us, I went with her to the doctor. You can see how these events brought us closer. By the way, the chemotherapy nearly killed her, literally, the first time it was given. They had to stop it before she was really finished, but it did the trick."

Minnett continues. "Cathy has always been a bundle of energy. She's been the chairperson of the committees, the room mother with the most creative projects, the hostess with the mostest. She is a fabulous mother. Her home is decorated to the nth degree but is warm and always open to friends and the children's friends. I once saw one of the boys carry a baby goat up to his bedroom during a birthday party, and she didn't blink an eye. She has always been positive and a tough cookie in adversity. This last cancer brought her to her knees, more than she had ever been."

During her most recent illness, Cathy wrote this letter to her many friends: "Every one of you has offered support to my family and me in some special way during this time of challenge. You are either one of the seventy-five who is scheduled to bring a meal to us, or you have driven my children to lessons and appointments, or you have written or e-mailed me, or sent me supportive Scriptures. You have visited me in the hospital, or you may have stayed with me through the night. Perhaps you have planned a birthday party for my children. Some of you have done it all. I thank you from the bottom of my heart . . . most of all for your friendship, your prayers, and your love. With my weakened energy level, I wanted to answer all of you fully, and I chose this letter as a way to do this."

Cathy is the young mother of three children, ages eight, seven, and four, and she has been stricken with cancer not once, but twice. The two forms of cancer are said by the doctors to be unrelated. Cathy says, "God just had a very unusual plan for my life."

Her letter continues, "My husband, Chris, is my mortal rock. When I am scared, he helps me pray. When I am tired, he stays alert for me. When I am hurting, he begs to take my pain. When I am distracted, he leads me back to my faith. I cannot explain the waves of emotion we have ridden together, but we have ridden every one hand in hand, as one. I thank God every single day that he gave me Chris."

Cathy goes on to speak lovingly of each of her children, the ways in which she has tried to explain her illness to them, and she says, "I have tearfully watched them pray, unprompted, on many occasions. . . . Sometimes I begin to hear their little voices in echo, and I become lost in thoughts of what-ifs and that is frightening for me. But I scurry to my faith that God will heal me. I go to him with every decision and every fear, and in many ways, he answers me."

Cathy has endured months of debilitating chemotherapy and several surgeries, but on a sweet note she writes, "On the day after my first surgery, I wanted my children to see that I was all right, and that I was not alone. They came dressed in doctor's scrub suits: green for Chris and Collier, and pink for Caroline. On the back the scrubs said 'Nurses in Training.' We all walked to see the newborn babies and prayed for them, and they toured the nurses' station and got chocolate milk!"

Cathy concludes her first letter, "I love you all and beg you to pray for me. Know that I promise to keep the faith and so I remain strong. I may have scars, but they are not on my heart."

Flash forward to October 2001. A large group dressed in pink and wearing "Race for the Cure" banners has gathered in downtown Shreveport. The crowd parts as a small and lovely mother, in jaunty cap and pink T-shirt, comes running in to the finish line, her shiny brown hair (a wig) swinging in a ponytail beneath her cap. She is breathless and exhilarated. Many, many of her friends are crying openly.

Cathy has not just run in this event, she spent almost every moment while she was well enough working and planning for it. This Race for the Cure event will raise thousands and thousands of dollars for cancer research. The love that has been shown to Cathy has overflowed into service. Now she is the wounded healer for others.

As I type this morning, my eyes are misty, and there is a lump in my throat. Cathy is by no means cured. Her lymph node was microscopically affected by the cancer, and her history and the form of cancer she has indicate that much caution is needed. She and her family must live day by day with their trust in God.

I am warmed by the love those around Cathy have shown her. Indeed, she is an extremely lovable person! And yet we are called to minister to all the sick and alienated as Christ did. Cathy is strongly living out these Christian and Ignatian principles of total faith and trust in God. In this trust, she moves forward in God's service.

She wrote to me recently in this way. "I don't want to be stoic or heroic, but I can honestly say that I feel extremely blessed to have experienced what I have. I strongly believe that God allows these circumstances to reveal areas in our lives that need spiritual pruning. As St. Paul says, 'He decided beforehand which ones were destined to be molded to the pattern on his Son, so that he should be the eldest of many brothers.' And," she continues, "God wants to use us to share his light with a dark world, as in the Gospel of Matthew: 'You are light for the world. A city built on a hill-top cannot be hidden.'"

"If you want to increase the strength of your muscles, you must increase the resistance on the barbell. So it is for any growth in life, if you don't experience resistance in life, you don't grow stronger. Hardships and adversities make us stronger people and create enormous opportunities for us to flourish." It seems that Cathy labors in her mission not counting the cost, even celebrating it.

My sister Minnett adds: "Cathy has beauty, wealth, intelligence, three of the most beautiful children God ever made, and an unbelievably handsome, kind, and strong husband. Yet, for the next three to five years she is living with a time bomb. If this cancer recurs, it could be in the breast area, but it would more likely be in the bone, brain, or liver. She goes in for a check-up every three months, but there is no way to monitor recurrence with 100 percent accuracy."

Cathy has resolved with St. Paul, "to run the good race to the finish." I admire her and the ways in which she has dealt with her tremendous obstacles and fears, turning them into opportunities for love and service. I would like to be more like her!

It is clear to me that with God's great grace Cathy is being molded into the image of the Son.

*As of August 2002, Cathy is in remission and feeling well! Praise God!

For Journaling and Reflection

❧ In what ways do your wounds and scars help you to reach out to others?

❧ Do you think that you would have been able to handle adversity such as Cathy's? Why or why not?

❧ Do you know people who have enormous problems and burdens yet manage to serve others? If so, describe these people and their stories.

❧ What helps to shore up your faith and trust in God—the type of faith that leads you to service?

36

Meeting Others
Where They Are

He then took a little child whom he set among them and embraced, and he said to them, "Anyone who welcomes a little child such as this in my name, welcomes me."

MARK 9:36–37

*P*rincipal Mary Moss sat at her desk feeling a frustration that she rarely showed to others. How long was she supposed to patch gaping wounds with tiny Band-Aids?

Standing before her was a little boy with a sullen and sad expression. Mary had been asked by the teacher to remove him from the room for a while.

"I can't teach," said Monica, the first-grade teacher. "He's muttering and moving his desk all around. The other kids can't concentrate at all."

"Sit down, Wally," said Mary now. "Tell me what's going on with you."

Mary knew only too well. This was the third Broussard child from Azalea Park that she had had at her school. Their mother stayed in her robe all day and watched television. It was obvious to Mary that she was not only depressed but probably using some drug. Men were in and out of the home. Drug deals and police raids were common occurrences.

Now Wally Broussard spoke. "I didn't have no bed. The baby daddy in my bed."

"And when did you eat last, Wally?"

"I couldn't go to breakfast. The bus was too late." Now the six year old began to sob. Mary opened her desk and handed Wally some peanut butter crackers. She buzzed her secretary, "Send a child for some milk, would you?"

Mary and I joked that I would write a book entitled, *There Are No Azaleas in Azalea Park*. This neighborhood of small, detached, government-supported houses was riddled with crime and violence. No one was in this neighborhood by choice, only because they had nowhere else to go. Many of the parents took drugs, and the children of our school were even physically affected by the inhalation of marijuana smoke, arriving to class hung over from its narcotic effects. Children came to school hungry and traumatized from fights and police actions during the night. Many of their uncles, brothers, and fathers were in jail. Some of the women turned to prostitution for money.

On a brighter side, Mary was a beacon of light in this community. She visited several times a week, securing birth certificates and shot records so that children could stay in school, getting children who needed special medications to the doctor, dropping off school supplies, looking for absent kids. I had worked for her for eight years, and I believed she was an angel from heaven. She spoke with gentleness. She knew that words could wound or build up adults as well as children, and she always chose her words with great care.

Mary made a decision. She needed to secure some funds, however meager, so that she and a colleague could start an on-site tutoring program in Azalea Park. She reached for the phone and began to make some calls.

Later that day, we chatted. "Angie and I are going to start tutoring in the Park three days a week," she said. "I'm getting a little money from Title I for Angie."

"Mary," I said, "how can you do that on top of your job? Where will you find the energy?"

"You may not believe it, but going to see these beautiful kids where they live is the best part of my day. It fills me. They love me with no conditions. They only want care and love in return. I can't not help them, and I must do everything I can."

Mary started her tutoring program. She or Angie usually sat on the outside steps of a home with a child, a paper, and a pencil. That was it. There weren't computers or fancy supplies; there wasn't even a family table to sit at. But they persevered. Some of the children's grades began to rise, and they were happier and calmer.

Very slowly, the attitudes of some of the parents began to change. Mary had never fussed at them or made them feel like bad people. She had just kept showing up and helping their children however she could. One day she went to tutor two brothers and found them sitting at the cleared-off kitchen table. They had sharp pencils and their books opened. The mother of the family offered Mary coffee! It was a breakthrough.

Other families followed suit. They were more and more impressed by the fact that Mary and Angie didn't quit, didn't condemn them, and showed no disdain. They just sat with children and read and watched as little hands formed the ABCs.

The city began to recognize Mary's work. One of the city councilmen held a reception for her and all the parents and children of Azalea Park who wanted to come. Mary was stunned when a bus went to pick up families and more than forty people were dressed and ready to go! Such a turnout was unheard of.

The councilman and others are now helping Mary get corporate grants to set up a center in Azalea Park. "But I won't stop going into the homes," Mary told me recently. "I don't want to lose what we are building up with these families."

Mary had found a way to shine a light into one of the darkest situations I had ever seen. I was overcome with depression when I visited Azalea Park, but Mary saw hope. She saw ways to bring that hope, and she did it humbly, faithfully, and out of nothing but pure love.

The company founded by St. Ignatius has brought love into many corners of the world. Their record has not been perfect. They sometimes fell prey to the prejudices and poor social practices of their day. Yet, they have repented and persevered. Just as Ignatius gave his last penny to the beggars in Rome, many a Jesuit has spent himself to the fullest in the spirit of Ignatius's words: "Take, Lord, receive my everything." Like my friend Mary, they have followed in the footprints of the pilgrim, himself a serving steward of God's love.

For Journaling and Reflection

❧ How do you believe God can help those oppressed by poverty or addicted to drugs?

❧ What are your reflections about Mary Moss's service to others?

❧ Are there any attitudes that are stumbling blocks for you in your life of service? If so, write about them now.

37

Not My Will, Yours

In a similar manner, when the enemy of human nature turns his wiles and persuasions upon an upright person, he intends and desires them to be received and kept in secrecy. . . . To use still another comparison, the enemy acts like a military commander who is attempting to conquer and plunder his objective. [He] sets up his camp, studies the strength and structure of a fortress, and then attacks at its weakest point.

IGNATIUS OF LOYOLA, *The Spiritual Exercises*

*C*asey Johnston's journey to becoming a deacon was difficult but rewarding. He studied for many hours and traveled faithfully to classes, giving up time with family and time for himself. Pursuing this discipline while running a small business was sometimes overwhelming. However, he planned to leave his business when his training was completed in order to work full-time for the church.

Now, a year after becoming a deacon, he was sorely disappointed. None of his plans were working out. The job he wished to have, as administrator of the parish, went to someone else. He felt that his ministry was being thwarted in many ways, as plans that he made did not receive needed approval. He began to spiral into anger and depression. He began to question God. "Why have you allowed me to be so stifled? Why don't people help me instead of placing roadblocks in my path?"

Casey's anger began to center on one person who he felt was especially blocking his path of service. He often thought about this person in anger, and so his resentment grew. It just wasn't fair! He had tried so hard to do the Lord's work, and it wasn't right that others were standing in his way!

Casey continued to take his walks very early in the morning, as he had done before his conversion. As he walked he often thought about the sad state of his ministry, a ministry for which he had held such high hopes. Even his singing of his original sacred music at Mass was discouraged. Not "congregational" enough. Well, he would not do music at all! That would show them.

As he walked, he could not help but be comforted a little by the beauty of the live oaks that surrounded Picard Park. Squirrels scuttled about, busily in search of acorns. The early fall day was warm, and speckled sunlight filtered through the trees. This was Cindy and Casey's home. He longed to serve God's people here. He was filled with sadness, and the bile of anger still rose within him. In fact, his anger was beginning to harden into hate.

As he walked quickly around the park's perimeter, he tried to dispel the energy of his resentment with exercise. Suddenly, he was stopped. It was happening for a second time! God was clearly speaking to him!

"Casey Johnston, listen to me! Do you think that you can start a ministry based on anger and disdain? The people I have put in your path for you to love, you are beginning to hate! Do you want to do my will or yours? Anger and hate are not the way. Love is the only way! Love them!"

Casey told me this story recently, as he recalled his early, struggling days of church work. "When God's voice spoke, all my resentment just fell away. It just fell away. I never felt it again! I had nourished my anger in secret, but God knew. Suddenly, it was all out in the open. And it was healed.

"As I started to work again with those people I had felt such anger toward, guess what? Their attitudes began to completely turn around! They saw the change in me, that I was committed to loving them. My work began to grow as I was given more and more creative responsibility.

"But despite my growing responsibilities at church, it became clear to me that God wanted me to stay with my chemical business. That was the message I wasn't willing to receive: God wanted me in the workplace. I have touched so many people there who would have never come near a church. And my workplace ministry has blessed my life beyond compare. It's not easy trying to keep everything balanced. But, that's not my job; it's God's job. I just do my best every day, fulfilling God's will, not mine."

It is impossible to read the life of St. Ignatius and wonder why he did not give up! He had to fight daily for his freedom to proclaim the gospel. He was misunderstood, told whom he could talk to and what he could say, and told what to wear and not to wear on three different traumatic occasions. He was imprisoned, called to account in courts, ridiculed, and demeaned on a daily basis. This, then, is the journey of a saint. We should not be too surprised or dismayed when our path of service is filled not with roses but thorns. We struggle with our own imperfections and limitations as we try to serve. Often we feel pulled in too many directions. Our energies fail us. And yet, the rewards do come. As Ignatius writes in his exercises: "In the case of those going from good to better, the good angel touches the soul gently, lightly, and sweetly, like a drop of water going into a sponge . . . the soul remains warm and favored with the gifts and after effects of the consolation."

And as George Ganss, S.J. tells us about Ignatius: "His mysticism was not confined to loving union with God in prayer but was oriented to execution and loving service."

I see Casey at least once or twice a week at choir practice and church. I can testify that his spirit is warm and favored with gifts. His is a life of loving service.

For Journaling and Reflection

❧ What roadblocks have been put in your path of service?

❧ Is resentment of others an issue for you? If so, write about how you might deal with it.

❧ How quickly or easily do you become discouraged? What helps you to overcome discouragement? What encouragement can you offer to others who are easily overcome by despair?

※ How do you "minister"—if that's possible—at your workplace? Describe how other people have ministered to you, at work or in other situations.

38

Hoarding Our Gifts

The third reason [for desolations in our lives] is to give us a true recognition and understanding, in order to make us perceive interiorly that we cannot by ourselves bring on or retain increased devotion, intense love, tears, or any other spiritual consolation; and further, that all these are a gift and grace from God our Lord.

IGNATIUS OF LOYOLA, *The Spiritual Exercises*

The caretaker at the Lafayette animal shelter greeted me cheerfully. "How can we help you this morning?" I was looking for a new pet.

We had two outside dogs at this time: Charlie, a young, active basset hound, and Eugenie, a frail, ill-tempered, and aging one. Eugenie could no longer play with Charlie, and he was not a very happy camper. I was searching for a new companion for him.

I spotted him almost immediately—a darling cocker mix, creamy gold with a thick, matted, and wavy coat and big amber eyes.

"Can I see this one?" I asked.

"Oh, that's M. J. He just came in. An elderly lady couldn't keep him anymore."

The little dog was sweet and docile, and I took him home. He touched my heart in an unusual way. I didn't really believe that he had come from the loving care of anyone, elderly or otherwise. For a long time, when I bent to touch him, he skittered away, his body in a cowed position. Also, he handled his food in an odd way. No matter how much was in the bowl, he would take a little bit and run far away so that no one could take it from him.

Time passed and things worked out just as we had hoped. I renamed the dog "Taffy," and he and Charlie became fast friends and inseparable companions. They play together all day long. Taffy gained weight, and we had him clipped to remove the matted hair. He has stopped cowering. The most touching thing about Taffy is that whenever he sees me, he runs pell-mell to greet me, as though I had been gone for days. He will do this ten times a day, whereas Charlie just looks up idly and seems to say, "Oh, it's just her." For Taffy, my entry into his sight is always a great event!

One thing has not changed about Taffy. He will always take one little piece of food and run away with it. This makes it difficult, for then Charlie eats the rest! We have tried a lot of things—separating their bowls more, staying with Taffy while he eats—but this seems to be a lifelong habit. Because of some early conditioning, he is so afraid to lose what he has that he misses out on other good things.

Well, dear friends, you are smiling because you probably can see where this bit is leading. God is pouring out so many good things at our feet, and often we cannot enjoy them. Because we are wounded, we run off, hide, and jealously protect what we have. The love that is meant to circulate freely among us in God's kingdom is stifled—is stopped at the source.

I know that when upsetting things happen and I am feeling "not loved" it is extremely difficult to show love to others. What is the answer? St. Ignatius tells me I cannot retain love and haul in graces by my own power; I can only have the courage to be receptive.

I read a quote once that I have not been able to find again. I don't think I will ever forget it. It said, "There is no greater tragedy than the folded-up life." What a vivid image, reminding us of the fetal position we long to adopt when we are in pain. Can I now offer myself to God to be unfolded again? Can I say, "God, I believe by faith that you love me and are recreating me, now use me"?

This is exactly what St. Ignatius did. He spun the dross of his early life into the gold of service, with God's help. He did not fly into sainthood on lifelong wings of perfection—far from it. His youth was marked with vanity, a flaming temper, and destructive celebratory excesses. Deep into the process of his conversion he could still be extremely stubborn and did not take good advice easily! I believe that because of this he often suffered much more than God intended. It was said of him, "Well, he is Basque, you know. What's yes is yes, and what's no is no!"

And yet, these very qualities in Ignatius were what God turned upside down and used mightily. We can see in the life of this saint that the answer to our wounds is grace. The answer to our selfishness is love. The answer to our fear is Christ himself, who did not spare himself but poured himself out as an offering of healing for us all.

For Journaling and Reflection

❧ Does being wounded block your service to others or your ability to receive God's gifts in any way? If so, describe how it does.

❧ What would a "folded-up life" look like? In what ways is your life like this? In what ways is it growing larger?

❧ How does your service flow out of God's love for you?

39

Songs of Love

*While I was going to the Chapel, and later at the beginning of
Mass and then during one part of it, I had much devotion, and
sometimes motion to weep.*

IGNATIUS OF LOYOLA, *The Spiritual Diary*

The darkness gradually began to leave me and the tears came.

IGNATIUS OF LOYOLA, *The Spiritual Diary*

$\mathcal{M}$ark Friedman and Janet Vogt are partners in the writing, teaching, and performing of liturgical music. I had
met them several times over the years and had finally arranged
for them to come to do workshops at our church.

Janet is petite and loving yet firm in her convictions about life
and music. Mark has a rich voice with which he has served communities in teaching and liturgy for many years. They are business partners and are both married to other people, but others
often don't realize this. Mark says, "I have been congratulated
on the birth of both of Janet's children, but I had nothing to do
with it!"

The weekend had spun by with cantor workshops, a traditional choir workshop, a children's choir session, and Masses. The group that I direct (once called the "youth choir" until someone sized up our ages!) is now referred to as the "folk choir." Our session was from six to eight o'clock in the evening, and I was excited about it. It was a privilege to have such talented folks working with our small group.

After they had been working on the group's technique for about an hour, I asked Janet, "Can we sing 'Make Us Holy, Make Us Whole' "? This is a song written by Mark and arranged by Janet. It is a beautiful prayer song that, in many ways, could be the theme of this book.

> *By your love, make us whole,*
> *May we rest in your compassion.*
> *Calm the lost, weary soul,*
> *in the warmth of your love.*
> *May your peace fill our hearts.*
> *May we know the love of Jesus.*
> *By your grace, you console,*
> *Make us holy . . . Make us whole!*

As Janet played the very notes she had written, Mark conducted our group in singing his song. A deep, warm feeling of Spirit descended on us all. As the choir sang their parts, Mark was obviously moved, and so was I. Then his eyes closed momentarily in pleasure as his hands beat time. As we all continued to sing, I prayed, "Oh, yes, Lord. Please make us Holy. Please make us Whole. Please heal our wounds so that we may serve you. Please lead us to be the people we are truly meant to be."

There were many healings and calls to holiness in Ignatius's life. During much of his *Spiritual Diary* Ignatius was struggling with a monetary question: Should he and the group he was founding have a steady income or not? Perhaps this issue represented one of his last surrenderings. He had begun his life in great wealth and stature. He had become a humble man of the cloth. Now, he was abandoning himself to God fully. No material goods could cushion his fall into God's providence, and many tears fell. Yet he saw his tears as a great blessing, as a grace.

Perhaps these tears were healing his fear of the future, for even great saints experience fear.

Our choir sang every verse of "Make Us Holy, Make Us Whole." As the last notes of the song faded, we all stood in silence for a long moment. I looked at Janet and Mark. "It's a great song," I said. "I hope we can always keep singing it."

For Journaling and Reflection

❁ What does the word *holy* mean to you? In what ways is holiness reflected in your life?

❁ In what ways do you long to experience more wholeness?

❁ How could wholeness lead to greater service in your life?

40

Life Is Good,
Especially the Healing Times

Come, bless Yahweh,
all you who serve Yahweh,
serving in the house of Yahweh,
in the courts of the house of our God.
Through the night watches,
stretch out your hands toward the sanctuary
and bless Yahweh.

May Yahweh bless you from Zion,
he who made heaven and earth!

PSALM 134

Christ's approach is the opposite of Satan's. Christ is the way,
the truth, and the life. Honesty, openness, and genuineness
mark his approach. We are urged to acknowledge the talents
we have been given. Instead of exaggerating their importance

to the point of self-possession and pride, Christ leads us to
thank God and recognize our talents as the gifts of the Trinity.
JOHN J. ENGLISH, S.J., *Spiritual Freedom*

I sit in my office at the end of the day, pondering the family picture of my brother and sisters, our spouses, our parents, and all my nieces and nephews. I know I am prejudiced, but I am somewhat taken aback by the beauty and diversity that I see in this picture: faces framed by red or brown hair smile back at me with black or blue eyes. The God of life keeps rewriting the recipe a trillion times to produce all this wonder, all this individuality. Life astounds me with its mystery and beauty!

I reflect also on this book and the time we have spent together. Even though I have not met you, gentle readers, I know you in my soul, as you now know me.

Most important, I hope you have come to know Christ, our Light, and his servant St. Ignatius of Loyola a little better. I hope you have come to know your own heart and God's healing work in you in a deeper way also.

The purpose of all my stories is manifold: I believe that we are all much alike in matters of the heart, in our fears and longings, our loves and losses, our struggles for faith. We can surely learn from one another, especially from those who choose to surrender to God. So much of our healing comes through this surrender. My purpose in writing these stories is also to put down in black and white the many ways that God is now active, loving, and healing in the lives of God's people. As Fr. Edward Beck states, "I have learned to trust stories to communicate spiritual wisdom, believing that stories relay spiritual and theological truths" *(God Underneath,* introduction). These stories illustrate that Christ's healing work did not stop with the Gospels and the Acts of the Apostles. It continues in your life and mine.

And I write these stories about woundings and healings because I have found that most often those who help with our healing have been wounded themselves. We are all broken in some way, and through these cracks in our hearts God's light shines, if we allow it to. As we travel our steep and winding roads, our compassion and love increase. What we have experienced we come to understand, sometimes after time has passed. When our understanding grows, often our love grows as well. And when our love grows, our service to others increases.

There is an amusing story about St. Ignatius of Loyola. It happened soon after his conversion, when he was in the heat of his new dedication. He was riding a donkey on a journey when he ran into a fellow traveler, a Moor. The Moor was of a different religion, yet he still had respect for Mary the Mother. He even stated that he could believe that Mary became pregnant with Jesus through the Holy Spirit. However, he told Ignatius that childbirth would have negated any virginity she might have had.

Ignatius let the Moor go on his way, but his heart became greatly troubled. He felt that he had let Mary down in not defending her honor, her perpetual virginity. He resolved to follow the Moor and to stab him with his knife! (In Ignatius, even converted, chivalry was not dead!) However, his doubts persisted. Maybe Christ did not want him to perform this violence. Tugged strongly in both directions, he decided to let the donkey decide! As he came to the crossroads, he released the reins. To the left was the large road leading to the town to which the Moor was headed. To the right was a smaller, rocky road leading away from this town. After some time, the donkey went to the right and probably rewrote church history!

It is an amazing story of a passionate, headstrong man who would have quickly died for his faith. However, it is also the story of a compassionate God who saw him safely home. His life of service was to be a far greater thing than his defense of Church dogma.

Do we dare to believe that this same God is leading our path, turning the donkey to the right? The truth is probably "sometimes." Sometimes our faith is strong and our hearts sing, and we are in what Ignatius termed "consolation." At other times, the road is dark, we are in desolation, and we feel that we are not riding the donkey—the donkey is riding us! At least, I feel this way sometimes. The trick is not to give up. The trick is to stay on the road until the light returns and we can again say, "Life is so good!"

Sometimes when we are in desolation we try to do too much. We try to compensate. We run wildly about, running from our pain when we are called to go inward. We are called to the feet of the God who heals. Only when we stop and spend time there can we go on. Then perhaps our service can spring from our love rather than the means by which we try to earn love.

I pray that your work with this book has been a time of becoming better acquainted with, and more attentive toward, the God who is always watching and who gives you gifts—of knowledge, peace, conviction, and healing. Whether we bring communion to the sick, sing in a choir, paint a picture, nurture a child, march in a protest, plan a potluck supper, work with the Sisters of Charity, or drive the carpool, we have an important place in Christ's kingdom of love. I hope that this healing walk with St. Ignatius has given you a little more hope and light.

For Journaling and Reflection

❧ You may have done quite a lot of writing as you worked your way through the stories in this book. If so, spend time over the next few weeks reading what you have written. You may want to continue this walk with St. Ignatius. Don't hesitate to seek out a spiritual director to guide you. You may have a desire to experience *The Spiritual Exercises* now. This would be a wonderful next step.

PRAYER TO THE GOD
WHO SERVES

Mother, Father God, I feel your presence
in every sunrise, in every sustaining meal,
in each smile on the faces of those I love.
You have served us all by sending so many gifts.
Thank you!

In gratitude, I want to share this felt love
with all those I meet.
Let my heart grow tender toward those
who are in any need.
Lead me to share without counting the cost.

May I use the talents you have sent me,
to comfort others and bring hope.
May I always sing your song of joy and peace.
Lift me up, my God!
And daily renew my strength.

MONTSERRAT

Ignatius, you speak to me
Of voices stirring deep within.
The dark spirit of anxiety,
Driving me to wanderings,
Leaving me cold and exhausted.

You hold, instead
The steady flame, consoling flame of joy.
Here it is, you say.
Take it. Hold it as your own.

How strange this is!
A twenty-first-century woman,
Clad in blue jeans, the daughter of Methodists,
Calling out to the passionate Spaniard,
Captain of a distant hill.

Ignatius, how did our paths cross?
When did the angels whisper your name?
You have championed my soul,
My Captain of a distant hill.

LYN HOLLEY DOUCET

EPILOGUE

Imagination is a gift from God—a reminder that we are made in his image. God moves in mystery and wonder. He speaks into the void and light breaks through.

TRICIA McCARY RHODES, *The Soul at Rest*

It is August 2002, and for a year I have been actively writing this book. I find it hard to let it go; it has become like a child to me.

My friend Yvette says that when her children began to leave for college she kept wanting to call them back. *Come back,* she said in her heart, *I may have forgotten to tell you something important!* Sending a book off to take a final form feels like that—I may have forgotten something. And I feel attached to you, the reader, who has sat patiently in my mind while I wrote. Yet now it is time to put all in God's hands (and into the able hands of the people at Loyola Press!).

This evening at seven o'clock, it became cool enough to sit outside under the trees. A gentle breeze blew, and I watched the birds coming and going in the greener-than-green trees. The earth quieted down, and peace settled in. I began to feel peaceful too, and hopeful that you will enjoy this book, benefit from it, and return to it and your journaling repeatedly over time. If through this process you feel that God has broken through to you in any way, then I am satisfied.

Remember that our journey is never complete on this earth; we keep learning and growing. And that's good news.

I leave you with joy and peace in Christ,

Lyn Holley Doucet

DISCERNMENT OF SPIRITS:
A WAY TO UNDERSTAND
OUR HEARTS

*I*n the course of reading this book you have encountered quotes from St. Ignatius of Loyola that mention both good and evil spirits. The work of Ignatius in the area of discernment (or understanding, judging) of spirits is one of his major insights.

I wanted to provide you with a short explanation of this area of spirituality. There are many books on Ignatian spirituality that will help you understand this concept if you decide to explore it further.

We as human beings are filled with a variety of thoughts, feelings, impulses, and plans. A cursory examination of our inner chatter reveals that we are creatures of both darkness and light, good and evil, love and fear. There is a duality within us of which Jesus often spoke. This is normal, part of being human.

Jesus explains these good and evil principles; for example, in Mark 7:23 he says, "For it is from within, from the heart, that evil intentions emerge." Jesus also states in John chapter 3, "In all truth I tell you, no one can enter the kingdom of God without being born through water and the *Spirit*" (italics mine). The kingdom of God is the place we want to live. We never want to act on our evil intentions.

It is therefore necessary, as we make both daily and long-term decisions, to sort through our thoughts, feelings, and options for acting. We have to decide if we are making decisions born of the good spirit or following an evil intention. As Christians we want to discover (or discern) God's will in our lives. We want to make choices that lead to the highest good for others and ourselves.

William Barry, S.J., says it this way: "The discovery of the religious meaning in one's inner experience is called discernment of spirits."

Acknowledging this religious meaning in life experiences helps us to find God in all things. We can be encouraged to encounter God at home, at work, in all of our relationships, in our leisure. There is no place that God is not. Further, God makes his presence known in our hearts.

Although this idea of discernment of spirits was in practice before the life of Ignatius, he gave impetus to the practice through his Spiritual Exercises. He identified good spirits as those movements (feelings, thoughts, revelations) within us that bring lasting spiritual consolation or solace and lead us to more light and more closeness with God. In Ignatius's worldview, these movements are caused by God and God's agents.

Negative or dark spirits lead us away from God and are present in desolation. In Ignatius's view these dark spirits come from the evil one. Desolation is marked by transient and fluctuating feelings and a lack of peace. God feels far away. St. Ignatius always advised against making major decisions in times of desolation.

Consolation always brings us closer to God and is marked by lasting peace and joy. We can experience consolation and sadness at the same time; for example, we may be sad about a loss, yet we experience the comforting presence of God. Pangs of conscience also come from God, and although they do not feel pleasant, their purpose is to help us reform and move closer to God. The following example concerns a man who was troubled by conscience and then moved toward God and a more consoling relationship with God and others.

Jerry spent several hours each evening watching television. He would come home after a tiring day at work and flop down, exhausted, on the sofa. His rationalization was that he needed TV to zone out and relieve the stress of the workday. Although he had three young children, he didn't want to talk to them or his wife a great deal in the evenings. He liked it when they sat quietly and watched TV with him. He would sometimes yell at the children when they didn't do this but made noise. His wife, Lois, often voiced her concern and anger about Jerry's behavior. She felt that the children needed more quality time with their father. She also stated that when she talked to him, he tuned her out and seldom answered. Jerry felt that he was too tired at night to do much of anything and that he deserved some downtime; after all, his father had always watched a lot of TV when Jerry was growing up, and he had turned out fine. What was the big deal?

As weeks passed, however, when Jerry attended Mass with his family and prayed in his pew, he thought about changing his habits. Sometimes the words of the priest's homily spoke directly to his heart, especially when Fr. Ken talked of love. Jerry felt that God was telling him that he must change and that it would be good for everyone if he did. Jerry realized that he felt somewhat depressed after an evening of television, and sitting on the couch didn't prevent his feeling tired the next day. Jerry was not feeling happy about things in general. Sometimes during Mass he would look at Lois and feel guilty that he left so much of the child rearing to her. He and Lois were drifting apart.

One evening, the next-door neighbor and his young son invited Jerry and the children to play baseball. Although he went reluctantly, Jerry was refreshed after the game. His children had laughed and enjoyed themselves. So had he.

That week during Mass, Jerry asked God for strength to be more committed to his family. He decided to play or read with his children at least three nights a week and to give his wife more of his attention. Jerry apologized to Lois, and to God, for his past behavior. He realized that his family was a gift from God that he had taken for granted. Now on many evenings the whole family plays a game or reads a Bible story. Jerry and Lois have instituted "date night" and are having quality time alone together also. The couple has grown closer, and the children are calmer and happier.

God communicated with Jerry's heart about a change needed in his life. Although the pangs of conscience were initially unpleasant, they led to conversion and consolation for Jerry. He feels more peaceful with his family at home and at church, and he feels closer to God.

Jerry could have gone in another direction and continued to defend his lifestyle choices. He could have become more and more angry when his wife said anything about his excessive TV watching or his ignoring the children. He could have tuned out the voice of conscience and even stopped going to Mass because it made him uncomfortable. If he had done so, the darker spirits would have won a victory in his life.

Discernment of spirits is a somewhat subtle art, and it may require the help of a spiritual companion. Your priest may be able to walk with you in your prayer life or recommend a spiritual director who has been trained in Ignatian spirituality.

I will say, finally, that Ignatius saw attention to movement of spirits as a way to bring faith into action by making godly decisions. It remains a way to participate with God in bringing his kingdom to life in our hearts, our families, our communities, and the world.

INSTRUCTIONS FOR GROUP

USE OF *A HEALING WALK*

WITH ST. IGNATIUS

A Healing Walk with St. Ignatius can be used easily in a prayer and/or discussion group. I have included a ritual to center the group and create a prayerful atmosphere. Members should bring their journals to the meeting. It works best if a leader is chosen for a given session. Leadership can rotate throughout the group, changing at each session or as often as the group determines.

This would be the order of the meeting

- beginning prayer ritual

- discussion

- prayers around the circle

- closing prayer

Beginning Prayer Ritual

Create a small altar on a table with a cloth, candle, or other special objects or plants. This altar can be very simple. Begin the ritual by gathering the group and moving into silence. The leader lights the candle.

Play quiet instrumental music, or sing a song or hymn together that sets the tone for reverence and trust.

During the music, you may choose to pass the candle around the group. The person holding the candle says a silent prayer and then passes the candle to the next person. This works especially well with instrumental music.

After the music, the group joins in this prayer: *God, we believe that you are moving in our hearts and bringing us to life abundant. As we gather today, we express our trust in your care. We ask you to be present to each member of our group. Let us unite in your peace and your love. Amen.*

The leader says, "Let us now offer each other a sign of God's peace and love." The members offer one another the sign of peace.

Pray together the Lord's Prayer.

Discussion

The group may want to discuss one or two chapters of the book at each meeting, depending on the size of the gathering.

A leader is chosen who will read journaling questions aloud from the book and invite participants to share some of what they have recorded in their journals.

The following ground rules should be presented at the beginning of a group's first discussion.

Do not share any information from these discussions with people outside the group. The questions in the chapters of this book are personal, and any sharing within the group is confidential.

Practice attentive listening as each person speaks. This can be a surprisingly difficult skill in our fast-paced world. We must ignore the thoughts of our own chattering minds to effectively attend to the person speaking.

Do not give advice. This is such an important precept for discussion groups of this type. No one should give advice to another or try to fix the person or problem.

Do not judge. Healing in the group comes through God and through our unqualified acceptance of one another. This is a time to lay judgments aside.

Give each person the opportunity to speak. It is easy for the more gregarious members to take up too much time. Be sensitive to one another. No one has to speak at a meeting, either; freedom is important.

Prayers around the Circle

Before closing the session, the group may want to pray together, to address various needs that have surfaced during the discussion.

There is a simple way to "pray around the circle." Each person (in no particular order—you don't have to literally go around the circle) can express one or more request to God. After each request (also called a petition), the group responds by saying, "Gracious God, hear our prayer."

Closing Prayer

The meeting can close with the following prayer or another of the group's choosing: *God, St. Ignatius of Loyola entrusted everything to your care. Let us imitate him as we move forward from this meeting, living only in your grace. Let us be kind to those we meet, and may we give our service to those in need, as Ignatius did. Care for each member of this group and each family represented here until we meet again. In Jesus' name we pray, Amen.*

The support of others during our spiritual journey can be so helpful! I hope that your group or club will benefit from this application of *A Healing Walk with St. Ignatius.*

BIBLIOGRAPHY

Barry, William. "Does God Communicate with Me?" *America,* 3 December 2001, p. 8.

Barry, William. *Letting God Come Close.* Chicago: Loyola Press, 1993.

Beck, Edward L. *God Underneath: Spiritual Memoirs of a Catholic Priest.* New York: Doubleday, 2001.

Cameron, Julia. *The Artist's Way.* New York: G. P. Putnam's Sons, 1992.

English, John J. *Spiritual Freedom: From an Experience of the Ignatian Exercises to the Art of Spiritual Guidance.* Chicago: Loyola Press, 1995.

Ensley, Eddie, and Robert Herrmann. *Writing to Be Whole: A Healing Journal.* Chicago: Loyola Press, 2001.

Fleming, David S., ed. *Notes on the Spiritual Exercises of St. Ignatius of Loyola.* St. Louis: Review for Religious, 1983.

Ganss, George E., ed. *Ignatius of Loyola: The Spiritual Exercises and Selected Works.* New York: Paulist Press, 1991.

Ghezzi, Bert. *Mystics & Miracles: True Stories of Lives Touched by God.* Chicago: Loyola Press, 2002.

Hardon, John A. *Retreat with the Lord: A Popular Guide to the Spiritual Exercises of Ignatius of Loyola.* Ann Arbor, Mich.: Servant Publications, 1993.

Hughes, Gerard W. *Seven Weeks for the Soul.* Chicago: Loyola Press, 1993.

Idigoras, Jose Ignacio Tellechea. *Ignatius of Loyola, The Pilgrim Saint.* Chicago: Loyola University Press, 1994.

Nouwen, Henri J. M. *The Inner Voice of Love: A Journey through Anguish to Freedom.* New York: Doubleday, 1996.

Rhodes, Tricia McCary. *The Soul at Rest.* Rockville, Md.: Bethany House, 1999.

Rupp, Joyce. *Your Sorrow Is My Sorrow.* New York: Crossroad Publishing, 1999.

Sanford, John. *Mystical Christianity: A Psychological Commentary on the Gospel of John.* New York: Crossroad, 1993.

Sklar, Peggy. *St. Ignatius of Loyola: In God's Service.* New York: Paulist Press, 2001.

Von Matt, Leonard, and Hugo Rahner. *St. Ignatius of Loyola, A Pictorial Biography.* Chicago: Henry Regnery, 1956.

Wansbrough, Henry, ed. *The New Jerusalem Bible, Reader's Edition.* New York: Doubleday, 1989.

Wicks, Robert J. *Seeds of Sensitivity: Deepening Your Spiritual Life.* Notre Dame, Ind.: Ave Maria Press, 1995.

Special note to reader: Quotations in this book's text that are cited from *The Spiritual Exercises, The Autobiography, The Spiritual Diary,* or personal letters were found in *Ignatius of Loyola, The Spiritual Exercises and Selected Works.* ed. George E. Ganss.